The Prometheus Release

A Tech Fable About AI Transformation, Software Leadership, and Building Systems People Can Trust

Jeremy Chan & Celia Liu

This is a work of fiction. Names, characters, businesses, places, events, and incidents are products of the author's imagination or used fictitiously.

This book uses British English spelling and usage to reflect its London setting.

First edition: June 2026
ISBN: 978-1-0667112-0-8

Published by Ceremy Digital Ltd
Official book page: https://prometheus.ceremydigital.com

Author’s Note

Before the story starts, one caveat.

Fiscari is invented, but the mood comes from real rooms. If you work around software and AI right now, you probably know the feeling already: a dashboard on the wall, a board conversation in the background, someone saying adoption looks great, someone else wondering whether great means useful, or only busy.

We compressed things. A real AI transformation leaks into support, sales, legal, finance, customer training, procurement, security, and all the dull places where serious change actually lands. This book keeps the camera mostly on David and the engineering leadership group. The calendar is tightened too. Problems that might unfold across months arrive in weeks. A few moments are heightened for entertainment.

The pressure is turned up so the machinery becomes visible. What we have tried to keep honest is the shape of the work: the misleading metric, the demo that gets applause before the discipline exists, the awkward question about who owns an answer after the answer has already sounded confident.

AI transformation is usually sold as a speed story. We think it is really a trust story. When the work gets faster, where does judgement live? Who can see it? Who can challenge it? Who signs their name to it?

Jeremy Chan & Celia Liu

Fiscari Org Chart

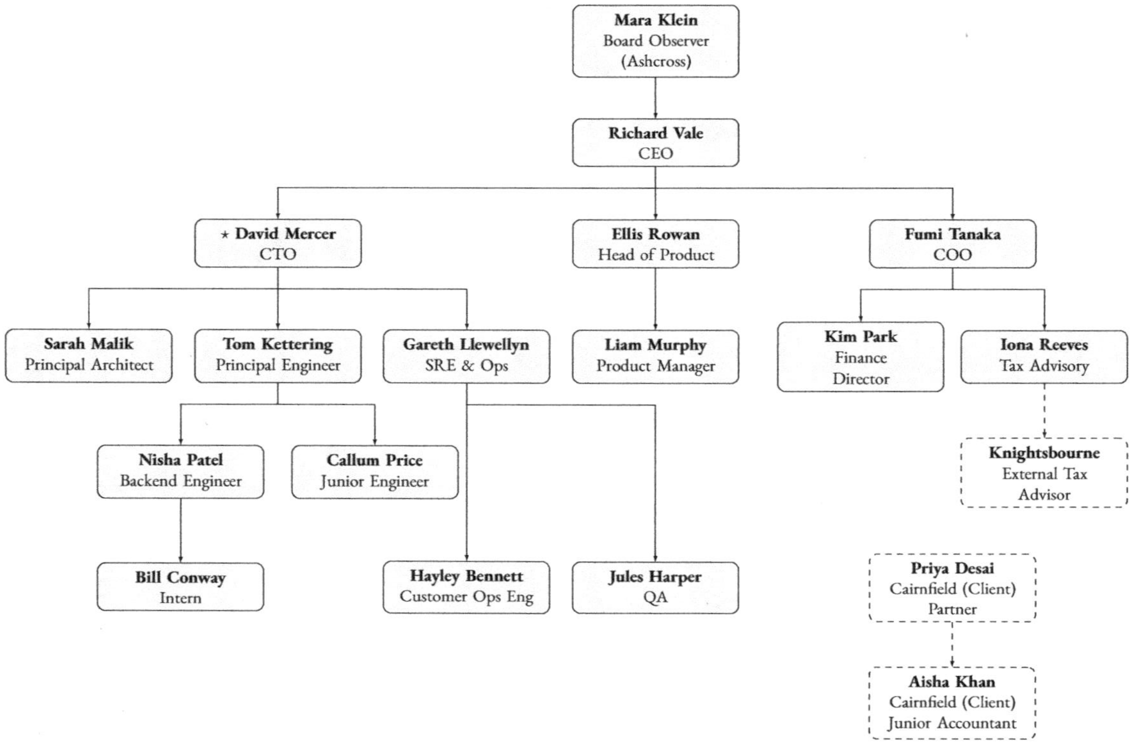

Email from CEO

EMAIL — RICHARD VALE

FROM: Richard Vale
TO: all-employees
SUBJECT: David Mercer and the Prometheus Release
DATE: 25 February

Team,

I am pleased to confirm that David Mercer is joining Fiscari as Chief Technology Officer, effective immediately.

The priority is simple: Prometheus Release. AI transformation is no longer a side programme; it is how Fiscari serves accountancy firms under pressure from payroll, VAT, Self Assessment, and landlord-client work. We need to help firms turn client evidence into reviewable tax work faster, without losing the judgement they are paid to stand behind.

David's mandate is to make that future real, move at market speed, and keep the judgement traceable enough that our customers can stand behind it.

Richard

Contents

It worked just long enough

for everyone to stop thinking.

Chapter 1
Unlimited Tokens

Monday, 25 May.

The rain had started before the bus reached Old Street. It turned the morning traffic into red smears, white smears, and cyclists riding on more belief than grip.

At 08:41, my phone said the migration was healthy. That became the first lie of the day before the bus had moved another metre.

My phone laid out the day with the cruelty of a tidy list. Investors at 09:30. Richard wanted the engineering floor glowing by then. Sarah Malik, the architect I trusted most, at 17:00 for her final handover.

Before the bus, Eclipse had already rejected the first version of the morning walk.

He is a Border Collie, which means any plan involving him is legally binding. At 07:12 he had planted himself between the front door and my laptop bag, wet lead in his mouth, negotiating with the calm focus of someone who had never seen a board deck and therefore understood priorities.

The rain turned the planned walk into six minutes around the square. A potty break pretending to be exercise. I dried his paws, filled the puzzle feeder, checked the walker's confirmation, and told him the transformation was healthy.

He looked unconvinced.

The navy technical trousers had survived the bus. They were clean and dry, which qualified as special for both London and the investors.

Usually I wore the London rain uniform: jeans, T-shirt, waterproof shoes, and a black waterproof North Face jacket. No umbrella. Londoners learned that early. Umbrellas turned inside out at crossings and turned busy pavements into fencing clubs.

I used to wear shirts.

At Goldman Sachs, I was a Tech Fellow in compliance technology. I questioned costly system behaviour, explained the reasoning, and handled the room afterward. Ten years of that. I spent a decade building trade-surveillance systems. It sounded grander than it was. Most days were about turning complex regulatory expectations into evidence that the firm had the right controls in place.

Fiscari hired me to do mostly the same thing with HMRC, His Majesty's Revenue and Customs, the UK tax authority that can turn a missing date, a pension threshold, or a domestic arrangement into a software defect with legal consequences. Only the acronyms changed. The boredom just wore a softer cardigan.

It was the kind of lie that came with a better title.

I took the bus because the Tube turned the morning into a geometry problem. You had to calculate around elbows, rucksacks, wet coats, and someone holding a flat white above your laptop bag with the confidence of a person who had never caused a production incident.

On the bus, I got 30 minutes to myself. A seat if London felt generous. A window if London felt cinematic. Time to read my messages, with enough rain on the glass to pretend the city had agreed to leave me alone.

My phone buzzed for the 17th time since breakfast.

The lock screen gave me the executive dashboard.

EXECUTIVE DASHBOARD

AI TRANSFORMATION PROGRESS `(vs pre-AI).`

PR VOLUME: `+340%.`

FRONTEND MIGRATION: `7.6% complete (on track).`

CODING-AGENT ADOPTION: `91%.`

TEST COVERAGE: `86%.`

MODEL SPEND: `84% of monthly budget.`

MONTH-END FORECAST: `110%.`

The numbers had been arranged to travel well. Coding-agent

adoption, for example, meant the percentage of users who had launched any coding agent in the past seven days. Whether that use had created value sat somewhere else, safely outside the Monday executive pulse.

PR volume was up, migration was ahead, and test coverage looked decent.

Only one line had the manners to look nervous.

Model spend: 84%.

That percentage was working hard. It was still May, investor-demo week was already pressing on the burn rate, and the forecast had no trouble finding 110%.

Three months earlier, the board had made me, David Mercer, CTO and handed me the Prometheus Release brief: lead Fiscari's AI transformation before investors decided we were the company being disrupted. My predecessor, they had concluded, had confused caution with strategy.

The first month was briefings, vendor review, procurement, and the discovery that many people could say governance while asking for permission to move faster.

Every vendor said they were the only platform built specifically for enterprise AI at scale. Three of them had the same slide. One of them had our logo on their website already. We had not given permission. They called it a partnership.

Two months earlier, the coding agent licences arrived, and Richard told the company to go crazy.

Go crazy was a sentence that should have required change-control approval.

The rollout looked serious enough to reassure the board and frantic enough to worry anyone reading invoices. Adoption climbed fast. Token spend climbed faster. Finance called it an innovation investment. Gareth called it a slow-motion arson attack with purchase orders.

Both descriptions were accurate.

Finance had flagged the same curve in March, asking whether the programme could slow down. Richard had called it a good challenge and accelerated anyway.

Unlimited tokens were never unlimited. They just meant finance had approved a number so large everyone stopped behaving like numbers existed.

The screen stayed green long enough for me to enjoy it for three seconds.

The bus crawled into the Old Street roundabout, which estate agents still tried to call Silicon Roundabout with straight faces. The junction was a wet loop of buses, scooters, cranes, startup offices, coffee queues, and people wearing backpacks with company logos.

Outside, a billboard slid past the window. It was eight metres wide and very confident.

> `SpritzTax`
>
> `See it. Say it. Sorted.`

Some copywriter had mugged a public safety announcement and taught it to invoice.

The smiling woman in the advert looked like she had never reconciled a VAT return while a client shouted about missing invoices. She held a coffee. Her laptop had no cables. Her desktop contained one window.

Nobody who worked in tax had one window.

That stung because we were trying to become the future the billboard had already sold.

Fiscari, where I worked then, was a 2,000-person UK tax, payroll, and accounting software company headquartered in the Tea Building[1], Shoreditch. That number included support, sales, implementation consultants, compliance, marketing, finance, and the people who knew which customers still faxed forms when frightened. Product and engineering was closer to 240 people. Small enough for a junior engineer to corner the CTO by the coffee machine.

HMRC collects taxes, enforces payroll and rules, and publishes enough guidance to make software companies confuse documentation with rocket science.

[1]A converted tea warehouse in Shoreditch, now a well-known office building for creative and tech companies.

We owned the boring middle. We sold to accountancy firms. Their accountants were our users; the landlords, directors, and sole traders were their clients, the people whose evidence arrived messy and whose tax position still had to be defended by a professional. The company's flagship product was called FiscariTax, because tax software companies liked names that sounded more orderly than the work.

We had a Java Spring backend that had survived 15 years of Java upgrades and governments discovering new ways to make ordinary income weird. We also had a C# desktop client built on Windows Presentation Foundation. It was Windows-only, packed with modal dialogues and hidden keyboard shortcuts. Customers trusted it because 15 years of tax judgement had hardened inside the buttons.

The split came from a 2014 merger nobody fully cleaned up: a C# desktop product grafted onto a Java tax platform with SQL doing peacekeeping in the basement.

The backend was a cathedral of accumulated judgement.

The frontend was a haunted filing cabinet with a year-2000 vibe.

The business logic lived in Java services, frontend event handlers, and stored procedures with names that sounded like warnings. Every strange branch had probably saved a customer once. Every strange branch now waited for a migration agent to misunderstand it.

The C# frontend was old judgement, stored in buttons.

The board had handed me that problem.

The old CTO had moved too slowly for a funding round that needed a future-tense product story, so the future-tense product story became my operating plan.

Richard Vale was our CEO, founder, and human keynote generator. He had neat hair and a quick smile. He also carried the ambient certainty of a man who could make a spreadsheet feel like a movement. He believed the future of accounting software was conversational. I agreed with him. Forms would die. Nobody wanted to fill in 487 boxes when they could ask a system what mattered and get an answer they could defend.

The hard part sat under the conversation.

Richard liked to start above it.

My phone buzzed again.

SLACK — RICHARD VALE (CEO)

```
RICHARD: hey David, investors 09:30. need floor
energy high. prometheus wall alive pls?
```

Prometheus Wall.

Richard named the programme after the Titan who stole fire from the gods and gave it to humans. He liked the fire part. He liked the stolen-from-gods part even more. Sarah pointed out that the myth also includes eternal punishment for reckless technology transfer, and Richard said that was exactly the kind of energy great brands need.

Prometheus Release was the migration programme. The old WPF desktop client, obsolete and Windows-locked, would become a modern web application that ran anywhere. Accountants could open it on a laptop, directors on an iPad, business owners on a phone at midnight. The backend stayed. The architecture stayed. The domain knowledge stayed. But the interface became conversational, responsive, and device-agnostic.

We installed a six-panel dashboard outside the main engineering floor. It showed migration burndown, deployment frequency, public token spend, PR throughput, team rankings, incident counts, and a rotating set of AI success stories. The numbers were large enough to satisfy passing investors, and the bright warnings carried judgement.

The Prometheus Wall had become our barometer. People glanced at it before they spoke, measuring the room's pressure before risking optimism.

I typed with one thumb.

SLACK — RICHARD VALE (CEO)

> YOU: on it

This was a lie in the limited operational sense. I was on a bus. The bus had moved another four metres. A red double-decker[2] ahead of us had stopped at an angle that suggested either a mechanical fault or a philosophical objection to traffic lanes.

I opened Slack.

The engineering channel was already awake.

SLACK — #ENGINEERING

> TOM: r2builder done w payroll ui batch 12 overnight. threepioreviewer says low risk
>
> GARETH: ai reviewer says low risk about everything
>
> GARETH: would call a gas leak minor ambience
>
> TOM: caught two null checks yesterday
>
> GARETH: heroic. give it a cape

I smiled. The room did not need my approval.

Gareth Llewellyn ran SRE like a border checkpoint. He was compact and unsmiling. He dressed as though a production outage might require him to crawl under a desk with a network cable between his teeth. Every token, tool permission, outbound dependency, and production credential passed through his suspicion field. He drank builder's tea[3] the colour of wet cardboard and treated polling loops as a moral failure. He also kept the site alive, which gave his opinions mass.

The bus finally escaped the jam and turned towards Shoreditch High Street. The Tea Building appeared through the wet glass, all brick and steel and expensive coffee, surrounded by improbable trainers and the concentrated glow of companies trying to become inevitable before their leases renewed.

[2] London's iconic two-level red bus.

[3] Strong, cheap tea brewed with milk, traditionally associated with construction workers and manual labourers.

Fiscari occupied three floors and one permanent sense of technical guilt.

I stepped off the bus and checked my phone before the door sighed shut behind me.

The same green story waited on my phone.

I crossed the road behind two founders discussing seed valuation and one delivery rider making a decision I would never put through risk review. Rain beaded on my jacket and ran straight onto my trousers. I had chosen this outfit. I reminded myself of that as a bus exhaled diesel and warm rain at knee height.

The office lobby smelled of espresso, wet wool, and new paint. Someone had installed a vinyl decal beside reception overnight.

> THE PROMETHEUS RELEASE
>
> AI-NATIVE TAX SOFTWARE FOR THE NEXT ERA

The typography was excellent. The owner field underneath it was blank.

I tapped my badge at the turnstile and took the stairs two at a time. The lift was full of people clutching laptops and performing the solemn silence of early meetings, until someone mentioned the weather and everyone briefly pretended to have a stake in it. Stairs gave me half a minute to think.

At Goldman, half a minute had once been all I got before a room decided I was the expensive kind of careful. I had spent nine months slowing an automation rollout because the exception trace was incomplete. I was right about the gap, and I was right so slowly that an outside review found a related blind spot before we shipped the fix. The programme was renamed, the lesson was filed under delivery failure, and my name stayed attached to the delay longer than to the warning.

Since then, speed had never felt neutral to me. When Richard talked about momentum, some part of me heard penance. I knew better than to confuse a fast story with a safe system; I also knew how it felt to be the person whose correct objection arrived too late to matter.

The transformation was working, and speed was the part everyone wanted to talk about.

Six months earlier, our frontend migration plan had looked like an archaeological project. We had hundreds of screens. Some contained business logic in event handlers written by people who now ran vineyards, cybersecurity consultancies, or posted on LinkedIn. Every estimate contained the phrase "depending on complexity," which meant the estimate was a ghost in formal clothing.

Then the coding agents arrived.

At first, we used them carefully for boilerplate, unit tests, and UI scaffolding. They caught null-handling mistakes and translated repetitive patterns from WPF into TypeScript. They also irritated senior engineers by cheerfully explaining code those same engineers wrote in 2014 on three hours of sleep and a dangerously optimistic ticket estimate.

It was real work, and it helped. Then the graph started moving.

PR volume went vertical. Cycle time fell. Junior engineers shipped features in days that would have scared them a quarter earlier. Support summaries appeared in seconds, and onboarding notes wrote themselves. Old backlog items vanished. Executives began using the words leverage and AI-native without punishment.

Richard saw the graph and saw destiny. I saw budget approval. Both interpretations had data.

On the third floor landing, I passed a poster from last year's compliance programme.

| EVERY CALCULATION NEEDS A TRACE

The poster had curled at one corner. Nobody had fixed it.

I tapped my badge and entered engineering.

Fiscari engineering used to sound like keyboards, coffee grinders, and Jira resentment. That day it sounded like a trading floor crossed with a hackathon where half the traders were watching other traders work. The air carried hot plastic from nine laptops running at capacity and the burnt-toast undertone of someone's second breakfast in the microwave. People stood in clusters and stared at coding agents typing for them. Screens showed diff views, design mocks, build logs, and animated dependency graphs. Someone had written TOKEN PARTY on a whiteboard and drawn a bar chart wearing sunglasses.

I left it there.

The Prometheus Wall dominated the far side of the room. Six panels of vivid green and live metrics.

PROMETHEUS WALL — LIVE

PULL REQUESTS MERGED THIS WEEK: `812`

AVERAGE REVIEW LATENCY: `19 minutes`

FRONTEND MIGRATION COMPLETION: `7.6% (38 of 500 screens)`

REPORTED TEST COVERAGE: `86%`

PRODUCTION INCIDENTS (LAST 30D): `0`

The zero-incidents tile had the clean shine of a kitchen before dinner service. It meant nothing was on fire yet, and said very little about where the matches were.

Tom Kettering stood in front of the Prometheus Wall with three monitors behind him and two laptops open on a standing desk. He was 28, fast, and funny. He was also structurally over-rewarded by the moment. His black hoodie said SHIP IT, THE MODEL SAID SO across the back. I'd approved that expense in a weak moment during a launch party, and now the slogan followed him like a prophecy.

His screen layout looked like a cockpit. Left monitor ran GitHub pull requests, centre showed the agent orchestration console, right streamed build logs.

He'd named his agents after Star Wars characters. R2Builder wrote code. ThreepioReviewer checked the diffs, anxious in tone but serene in liability. YodaTax played archaeologist. It connected to company wikis and support tickets, to the collective memory of engineers who had left but still haunted the code. LeiaScribe wrote docs that sounded calmer than reality. There was also one called DeathStar, which, despite the name, existed to stop things from blowing up production.

Tom saw me and grinned.

"Morning, boss. Look at this."

He pointed at the console.

"I just let R2Builder chew through payroll batch 12 overnight. 81 files, two null checks from ThreepioReviewer, one binding fix, release notes from LeiaScribe, and the branch compiles."

"Overnight, you slept?"

"Like a baby."

"While the agents worked?"

"Exactly. Delegation."

I stepped closer to the monitor. The diff was large. Too large for a human review before lunch. Most of it looked mechanical. The diff was full of TypeScript components, state handlers, API stubs, validation messages, tests, and snapshots. All of it generated.

I scanned filenames.

```
PayrollHolidayRulesPanel.tsx
PensionOptOutSummary.tsx
StatutorySickPayEligibility.tsx
```

The old WPF screen names sat behind them in comments like fossils.

"Who owns the payroll eligibility review?"

Tom clicked twice.

"ThreepioReviewer marked it low risk. It says the migrated component only changes presentation state, tests are green, and the diff is basically a UI map."

"Is it really?"

He gave me the look high-output engineers give managers who slow down good news.

"The tests pass."

The answer moved the meeting along and missed the question I had asked.

The distinction stayed small and inconvenient.

I also knew Richard would arrive with investors in 20 minutes.

"Get Hayley to spot-check the payroll eligibility paths," I said.

Tom nodded and typed a Slack message.

Compliance had become fast and frictionless, the modern ritual of being sensible.

Callum Price appeared beside us with a notebook held against his chest. He was a junior engineer by title, not by temperament.

He was 26, thin, and sharp-eyed. He was new enough to Fiscari to bring actual paper into a live architecture argument. I respected the courage.

Fiscari liked to say every engineer should feel comfortable joining a conversation with the CTO, even in front of the Prometheus Wall, even when the room was moving fast. It was one of the better parts of the culture when it was true.

"Tom, quick one. The migration agent moved the director NIC[4] edge case into the shared eligibility helper. Do we know why the old code treated newly appointed directors differently after PAYE[5] correction imports?"

Tom did not look away from his screen.

"Did you ask YodaTax?"

Callum hesitated.

"I did. It said likely historical compatibility."

"There you go."

Callum waited for more.

None arrived.

Tom had already moved into another terminal pane.

"Tom."

He looked up.

"What?"

"Likely historical compatibility tells him where to dig. It does not tell him what happened."

"Sure. But it gives him the direction. The agent can trace references."

Callum said, "It found three references and two contradicted each other."

Tom smiled.

"Welcome to Fiscari."

The joke worked. People nearby laughed. Callum smiled because junior engineers learned quickly which uncertainties could be made social.

I gave an answer with just enough responsibility to let the

[4] National Insurance contributions, payroll deductions that help fund UK state benefits.

[5] Pay As You Earn, the UK payroll system for collecting employment tax.

room keep moving. "Pair with Hayley for 20 minutes. If the rule affects calculation, tag tax for domain review."

Callum nodded and left.

Tom raised both hands.

"See? Human in the loop."

"The loop is getting large."

"The loop is getting productive."

He turned back to the monitors. The build passed. A small green tick appeared beside the branch.

A bright Mario coin sound pinged from the Prometheus Wall.

I looked up.

"What the heck was that?"

Tom did not even turn around.

"Bill made it. Intern."

The room cheered.

Engineers were rational until the machine gave them a green tick. Then we became villagers at a harvest festival.

◇ ◇ ◇

Sarah's desk was the only quiet place on the floor.

It sat near the window, half-cleared, with two cardboard boxes underneath and a monitor displaying a plain text file inside Emacs. People used to hate pairing with her because of Emacs. It felt archaic in the age of IDEs, all grey buffers and key chords that looked like a pianist losing a fight.

Then terminals became cool again.

Sarah did not change. Fashion looped back around and congratulated itself.

Her desk had none of the usual camouflage: stickers, action figures, or an ironic desk plant with a name. Sarah had always regarded workplace whimsy as an availability risk.

She was Fiscari's Principal Architect until 5 p.m. Then she would become a leaving-drinks calendar invite.

I found her reading code.

Working with Sarah was not the problem. She was a genius

and knew the system inside out. The problem was what it cost to be near that much unfiltered accuracy for years. Sarah trusted written systems more than spoken confidence. She kept notes the way other people kept memories, which made her difficult to impress and very hard to fool. A code review with her could start with a naming nit and end thirty-seven minutes later in a payroll regulation from 2013. Every junior engineer's nightmare was a pairing session with Sarah and a branch they thought was finished.

"Morning," I said.

She lifted one hand without turning, greeting optimised for throughput. On her screen was an old Java class. 1,200 lines. Tax year branches. Comments that began with FIXME and then explained the entire reason the fix never happened. A method name long enough to qualify as documentation and still fail.

"Enjoying your last day?"

"Immensely."

"That looked sincere."

"I practised."

I stood beside the desk and her boxes. The top box contained two notebooks, a battered copy of the HMRC developer guide, and a mug that said I HAVE CONDITIONS. She hadn't packed the architecture diagrams from the wall behind her. They were taped up in overlapping layers. Payments. Payroll. Self Assessment[6]. The arrows formed a black-ink weather system.

"You saw the dashboard?"

"Everyone saw the dashboard. The dashboard is visible from space." A few people on the floor laughed. Sarah didn't turn around.

"It is good, though."

She scrolled. "It is green."

"Green is adjacent to good."

"In the same way a glossy pitch deck is adjacent to a legal opinion."

I laughed once. She didn't. She had a talent for removing the

[6]The UK's system for individuals to report their own income and calculate tax due, filed annually by 31 January.

foam from conversations. That used to irritate me. Then I became a VP and discovered foam could fill entire quarters.

"Come on," I said. "Even you have to admit something is working."

She stopped scrolling. That should have warned me.

Sarah turned her chair. Dark circles. Loose posture. No performance, no start-up theatre. She looked like someone who had spent years holding a map while everyone else accelerated into fog.

"Something is working," she said. "I'm not sure it's engineering."

It was the sort of sentence executives could carry between rooms, which was exactly why it damaged things.

"Someone is going to turn that into a quote in a resignation post."

"I am already resigning. The channel is available."

"You know what I mean."

"I do."

She turned back to the Java class.

"The agents are useful, David. They write boilerplate and summarise mess. They give people a way into old code and reduce blank-page fear. I use them."

"You use them?"

"Of course."

"You never mention that."

"People become strange when you give them evidence against the version of you they made up."

I absorbed that. Fair. The word sat there, accurate and inconvenient.

"Then what is the issue?"

She pointed at the Prometheus Wall. "Your metrics measure output. They do not measure understanding."

"Understanding is hard to measure."

"So is tax compliance. We still try."

A cheer rose from Tom's cluster. Another build passed. The Prometheus Wall updated. Pull requests merged that week became 813.

Sarah watched the number change.

"Reading is the bottleneck now," she said.

"Review latency is down."

"Review latency measures how quickly someone clicks approve."

"We have AI review as a first pass."

"The AI reviewer reads what we generated: code, comments, tests. It produces generated confidence. The loop has grammar. Independence is missing."

I wanted to argue.

I could assemble the argument easily. Delivery had improved. Customers needed modern workflows. The board expected visible movement and engineers liked the tools. The old process gave us two-year migration plans and meetings about meetings. AI had changed the economics of software creation, and a company that refused to adapt would get eaten by a competitor with better billboards.

The argument came easily because most of it was true.

I like true arguments. They save time.

"We still have humans approving," I said.

"Tired humans approving larger diffs faster."

"That sounds like a capacity planning issue."

"It is a craft issue."

The word craft carried more weight than I expected. Executives used craft in all-hands speeches when they wanted to soften the request for more velocity. Sarah used it like a structural term.

"Typing is the visible part," she said. "The craft is deciding the constraints before anyone writes."

I glanced at the clock. 09:23. Seven minutes until Richard. Seven minutes until investor theatre.

"I wish you had put this in your full architecture handover."

"I did."

"The document is 70 pages. I read the summary."

"The system is 15 years old."

It was accurate, but unhelpful in the moment.

Her screen showed a comment block from 2016.

```
/**
 * Intentionally complex
 * Handles pro-rata director NIC earnings
periods
 * after PAYE/RTI correction imports
 * See HMRC NIM12022
 **/
```

I read it twice.

"Is that the thing Callum just asked about?"

"Probably."

"YodaTax called it likely historical compatibility."

"That phrase means the model found a tombstone and called it landscaping."

I took out my phone and messaged Hayley.

SLACK — HAYLEY BENNETT (CUSTOMER OPS ENG)

> YOU: `can you pull sarah into callum payroll edge-case review before lunch`

Hayley replied in six seconds.

SLACK — HAYLEY BENNETT (CUSTOMER OPS ENG)

> HAYLEY: `already did`

Good enough, whether it came from Hayley or from Hayley's agent. I took the win and kept moving.

Chapter 2
The Demo

By 09:30, Richard arrived with investors, two board members, and a smile that had closed funding rounds in rooms with no working product. He wore a navy suit with white trainers and no visible anxiety. At forty-something, he still had the founder metabolism: too much coffee, too few pauses, and a gift for turning every corridor into a stage. An office tour became a product launch around him. He remembered names while walking and touched shoulders at exactly the frequency that made people feel selected rather than managed.

The skill was enviable. It also made me check the exits.

The Prometheus Wall refreshed as he crossed the floor. Another green tick appeared. The timing was perfect enough to make a decade near compliance systems distrust the animation.

Beside him walked Mara Klein from Ashcross Ventures, our lead Series E investor. Small, precise, dressed in grey wool that cost more by refusing to announce itself. Before VC, she'd founded a compliance automation company and sold it to a US payroll platform. She had written enough production code to distrust demos on principle. She watched screens instead of faces, reading the office the way engineers read logs: timestamps first, confidence last. Professionally inconvenient.

Richard clapped once. "Here we are. The Prometheus Release."

The floor lifted its head. He gestured at the Prometheus Wall.

"This is what happens when you remove the cost of translation. Ideas become software."

A great line. I'd heard it eight times, and it still worked.

Mara studied the dashboard.

"PR volume up 340% against your pre-AI transformation baseline."

"Correct," Richard said.

"I will want the raw PRs behind the summary," Mara said.

Richard smiled with only the executive muscles.

"Of course."

I noted it. Of course was the first line in too many diligence problems.

"How are you preserving review quality?"

I stepped in because that was my department and because Richard would answer a different, prettier question.

"Mara, the speed is real, and the controls have to be real as well. We use agent first pass for mechanical issues, human owner review for system impact, domain review for calculation paths, and SRE gates on production permissions and dependencies."

The intended state contained enough truth to survive a tour.

Mara pointed to another panel.

"18,000 generated tests. 86% reported coverage."

"Yes," I said. "Across migration and regression coverage."

"Generated from what source?"

It was the right question. Much too precise for 09:34 with investors watching.

"Code structure, existing snapshots, historical ticket examples, and test patterns from the target modules."

"Business rules?"

"Where documented."

She waited.

There was a whole company inside those two words.

Where documented.

Some rules were documented in wiki that had last been edited in 2019 by someone who no longer worked at Fiscari.

Some were documented in tests.

Some were documented in the memory of people standing too close to the coffee machine.

The rest were documented in customer anger.

Richard moved before the pause became a finding.

"Let me show you the energy on the floor."

He guided them towards Tom.

Tom was demo-safe in the way fireworks were wedding-safe if everyone stood far enough back. He could make hard things look easy. He could make impossible things look scheduled.

"Tom runs one of our highest-velocity AI teams," Richard said.

Tom swivelled around. He was wearing a black hoodie whose sleeves had lost a fight with anxiety chewing. His hair pointed in several operational directions. So did his commits.

"Morning. Welcome to the circus."

Mara gave the joke half a millimetre.

Richard said, "Tom, show them the migration cockpit."

Tom tapped a key. The agent orchestration console filled the centre monitor with a dark grid of queued jobs, repository paths, token counters, tool permissions, and animated status badges pretending that model uncertainty could be made rectangular. It showed which AI jobs were running, what code they could see, and which tools they were allowed to touch. Four model workers sat in the queue: R2Builder, ThreepioReviewer, YodaTax, and LeiaScribe. They looked less like names than a licensing dispute.

"I break the WPF screens into bounded jobs," Tom said. "R2Builder drafts the React, ThreepioReviewer checks common failure modes, YodaTax pulls the domain context, and LeiaScribe kicks out the notes. Humans pick up the branch with the boring work already done."

"Humans where?" Mara asked.

Tom pointed at himself.

"Here."

A good answer, and incomplete enough that I stepped in.

"And in code ownership," I added. "No generated branch merges without named human accountability."

Gareth coughed from somewhere behind us.

I chose not to identify the cough as dissent.

"And the required GitHub check stays red unless that owner is present," I said.

Gareth stopped coughing.

For SRE, silence counts as applause.

Tom showed a payroll screen before and after migration. The old WPF client appeared first, all grey boxes and tiny labels, with a modal that looked like it had been designed under fluorescent duress. Then the new React view appeared. The layout was clean and search was fast. Validation appeared inline, labels were accessible. It looked modern because it was modern.

The investors shifted closer to their screens.

Richard lived for that moment.

Tom opened a debug panel.

> `The migration preserves the original eligibility logic while improving presentation structure and validation clarity.`

I read the sentence.

Preserves original eligibility logic might be true.

A branch in the old Java code said newly appointed directors needed special treatment after PAYE correction imports. YodaTax had summarised something similar as historical compatibility. Hayley had already pulled Sarah into the review. The branch had not merged.

In the room, that passed for containment.

Mara asked, "Can I ask the system why the original eligibility logic exists?"

Tom's fingers hovered above the keyboard.

His hand stalled above Enter.

The debug panel had a chat interface bolted to the trace view. Then he typed into it.

> `Explain why pro-rata director NIC earnings periods differ from standard employee NIC calculation.`

YodaTax streamed an answer.

> `The system appears to preserve a historical compatibility path for pro-rata director NIC earnings periods, likely related to legacy PAYE correction import workflows. The migrated component maintains the same conditional structure to avoid behaviour changes.`

Mara read it.

"Appears. Likely. Legacy."

Three words. She selected them like evidence bags.

My phone buzzed.

TEXT — FRANKIE (DOG WALKER)

```
FRANKIE: Hey! Just to let you know Eclipse got
into a bit of a scrap with a Labrador at
the park. He's fine! The Labrador started it.
Eclipse was very persistent though.
```

I turned the phone face down.

Sarah was already looking at me.

I had two problems I could not fix in the next thirty seconds.

Tom said, "Right. It flags uncertainty. Good behaviour, provided it can back the flag up."

Mara said, "Can it cite the case or rule?"

Tom typed again.

The model thought.

Thinking was the animation we showed while the probability engine spent money.

It returned a reference to NIM12022.

My shoulders released one centimetre.

Then it returned a second reference to SAM-7438.

I had never heard of SAM-7438.

Sarah had.

She appeared beside me with Callum and said, quietly, "That second one is a pension import incident. Same customer."

Tom heard her.

"It retrieved a piece of nearby information. Easy fix."

Sarah said nothing.

Silence was her most expensive tool.

Tom looked back at the Java path and lost his speed for the first time that morning.

The method was 230 lines long, with three nested date branches and a comment from 2017 that said "temporary until HMRC clarification". His fingers hovered over the keyboard. The agent could summarise it. Tom could ask it to explain the branch.

What he could not do quickly was trust the explanation.

This was the part his hands slowed for.

The old code did not care how clever he was.

Richard moved again.

"This is the leverage," he said. "The workflow surfaces uncertainty while the work is still moving. Humans stay accountable, and the speed lets us learn where the old product is hiding risk."

He was right.

He was also stepping over the interesting part.

The machine finding something was not the interesting part.

Whether it knew what it had found was.

Mara turned to Sarah.

"You are?"

"Sarah Malik. Principal Architect."

Sarah was tall and still. She was severe in the way clean code is severe: black jeans, black jumper, Apple Watch, and activity rings closed every day with the same grim consistency she brought to architecture review. Her face gave away almost nothing until someone said something technically careless, then one eyebrow moved a millimetre and the room lost temperature.

"What do you think of this workflow?"

Richard watched Sarah's face instead of Mara's. Sarah looked at the dashboard, at Tom's agents, then at me.

"It has value," she said.

Richard smiled. Too early.

"Useful tools need sharp boundaries."

Mara nodded. "Do these have them?"

"Some."

One syllable. Catastrophic efficiency.

Richard laughed as if this was charming. "Sarah is our resident sceptic. Every strong engineering culture needs one."

Sarah looked at him. "Every strong engineering culture needs more than one."

I stepped in because my job occasionally involved preventing board-level poetry from becoming a wound.

"Sarah has been leading our architecture standards for years,"

I said. "Her point is exactly why we are pairing the migration work with domain review and SRE controls."

Sarah looked away first. Gift accepted.

Mara watched the exchange. She missed nothing. Investors never did in the first meeting. Later, after the paperwork, they could become wonderfully surprised by things they were paid to notice.

Richard guided the group to the meeting room.

◇ ◇ ◇

The floor tour had been the warm-up. The formal executive AI steering meeting started at 10:00.

Winter is Coming had glass walls, a long table, and a view of Shoreditch rooftops shining wet under low clouds. The glass held the rain sound out and the room's own heat in: coffee, dry markers, and the faint electrical hum of two projectors running. The smaller room next to it was *The Red Wedding*. Someone had named the meeting rooms after television quotes during a culture refresh and nobody had the courage to reopen the decision, so we continued to discuss multi-million-pound funding rounds in places named after fictional massacres.

Someone had arranged pastries on a tray. Nobody ate them. Pastries in investor meetings were load-bearing decoration. Tom took one. Tom had never read a term sheet.

The room had two clocks: one on the wall, and one in Richard's head. Only one of them could be seen by engineering.

I sat between Richard and Gareth. Sarah sat at the far end. Tom stood by the screen with a clicker, bouncing on his heels.

Gareth had brought his mug into the investor meeting. Nobody said anything. The mug said ALERTS ARE NOT NOTIFICATIONS. Nobody in the room knew the difference. Gareth had stopped explaining it in 2019.

The first slide said:

> PROMETHEUS RELEASE
>
> FROM LEGACY TAX SOFTWARE TO AI-NATIVE OPERATING SYSTEM

Operating system.

We make tax software.

Language inflation was a known side effect of fundraising.

Tom presented the metrics well. He was clear and fast, honest in the way high-speed people were honest. He told the truth visible from his cockpit.

"We have agents on migration, review, test generation, release notes, and support summaries. The big gain is parallelism. People stop waiting for blank-page work. They get first drafts, diffs, summaries, and suggested tests. Human engineers spend more time steering."

Mara asked, "Steering what?"

Tom said, "The agents."

Sarah looked down at her notebook.

I knew what she wrote before I saw the pen move.

Steering was doing work.

The word sounded controlled until someone asked for the steering column.

Tom continued.

"The migration backlog is finally moving. The old WPF client has been our anchor for years. With model-assisted translation, we can convert common patterns at scale."

He showed a beautiful graph: up and to the right where it should rise, down and to the right where it should fall, crimson where it needed urgency, green where it wanted applause.

Richard glanced at Mara during the green sections.

Mara took notes during the grey ones.

Gareth raised a hand.

"Model spend is at 84% of monthly budget because I increased cache reuse and killed three teams' habit of sending entire repositories into long-context prompts every afternoon. They were paying the model to reread the same codebase until the invoice became a weather system. Without that, the month-end forecast would be worse than 110%."

Tom said, "Those prompts worked."

Gareth turned his head slowly.

"So does pouring petrol on damp wood if your only metric is whether the smoke gets bigger."

Richard's smile stayed in place. Tom stopped bouncing.

I said, "Spend controls are improving. Gareth's team is adding model routing next sprint."

Gareth grunted. This counted as alignment.

Richard took over for the final section.

He stood. He always stood for vision slides.

The screen changed to a mockup labelled Ask AI. An accountant asked a client's tax question in plain English. The system was not supposed to answer like an ordinary chatbot with a cleaner voice and a worse liability model. It started from the selected taxpayer profile, pulling filing history and property records, then asked for missing information and gathered evidence. A human reviewer would still have to decide what the draft workflow fields meant. The same question could produce a different path for a different client because the client's facts changed the answer.

The woman in the mockup asked: "What does my client owe this year?" The system responded with a clear, confident summary.

Nobody had modelled the follow-up question.

It looked excellent.

The mockup bypassed the ugly things we still had to solve: identity, permissions, audit trails, statutory citations, liability boundaries, and the old SQL schema that stored dates in three formats because the 2012 payroll import had opinions.

The demo worked because it showed none of that.

Richard gestured at the screen.

"This is the future. No accountant wondering which box matches the real client question. Fiscari becomes the interface between human intent and statutory complexity."

It was a good sentence. I made a note to put it in future release notes.

Mara said, "Can you ship this?"

Richard turned to me.

There were correct answers, true answers, and useful answers. Leadership often asked you to pick one under fluorescent lighting.

"We can ship a controlled Ask AI beta," I said. "Limited firms. Rental-property questions first. Evidence capture, draft classification, citations, and human review on every output. No filing."

Richard nodded as if I had said yes.

Mara didn't nod. She'd heard the soft spot.

"By when?"

Richard had already spent the yes. Mara was pricing the caveat.

Sarah's gaze reached me from the far end. I ran through the constraints. Architecture review had to come first. Deterministic services had to sit under the conversational layer. Tool choice, escalation policy, and missing-data handling were business logic, not UX polish. All true. All solvable if we kept the beta narrow.

"Mid-summer is plausible for Ask AI if we keep the beta narrow."

Plausible sounded careful. Richard heard permission.

Richard smiled. "Exactly. The market has moved. We move with it."

Mara wrote something down. The rain hit the glass behind her in thin diagonal lines.

Richard clicked to the final slide. It showed the Fiscari logo, the FiscariTax wordmark, the Prometheus Release codename, and one sentence in large type.

> THE DEMO SETS THE PRODUCT NOW.

He said it aloud. "The demo sets the product now."

Nobody challenged him, including me.

The dashboard outside the room updated again. Another pull request merged. Another green tick appeared. The Prometheus Wall glowed through the glass like proof.

Sarah had closed her notebook.

The first red metric of the day.

Chapter 3
The Agents

The formal meeting ended at 10:47. Richard left first because vision travelled faster when it did not have to carry its own laptop bag.

Mara Klein stayed behind for another 12 seconds. She looked at the final slide again, then through the glass wall at the Prometheus Wall dashboard, then at me with the professional calm of a person deciding whether the new CTO understood his own machinery.

"Send me artefacts," she said.

"Yes."

"Actual artefacts. PRs. Reviews. Test evidence. The migration plan behind the graph."

"You will have them this afternoon."

I heard myself use the useful voice, the one that turned uncertainty into an afternoon calendar.

Manageable, because nothing had technically broken.

Mara nodded once and followed Richard out of *Winter is Coming*. Gareth took a pastry from the tray, wrapped it in a napkin, and put it in his jacket pocket.

"Emergency ration?" I asked.

"Evidence."

"Of what?"

"That this meeting contained food and nobody had the judgement to eat it."

He left.

I caught him at the door.

"Next investor meeting, tune down the negativity by 10 percent."

Gareth's jaw moved once. Hard.

"I was saying the truth."

"I know. Sometimes we keep some truth to ourselves until the room can survive it."

"That sounds unhealthy."

"It is called sequencing."

Sarah remained at the far end of the table, writing in her notebook. Actual pen. Actual paper. She underlined something twice. This worried me. Sarah single-underlines for emphasis. Double-underlines for future indictment.

"What did you write?" I asked.

She closed the notebook.

"Nothing that helps you by this afternoon."

"That narrows it down."

My phone vibrated.

SLACK — RICHARD VALE (CEO)

> RICHARD: `it went well. good job`
>
> RICHARD: `need to make sure we have the evidence she asked for`
>
> RICHARD: `let me take a look before you send it pls`

Richard at his best and worst in three lines: warmth, escalation, control.

The dashboard was not false. I used that defence at the time.

It was selectively true, and that was the dangerous kind.

Mara had asked for PRs, reviews, test evidence, and the migration plan behind the graph. We had all four. We also had a review backlog, policy pages that existed mainly as headings, and a growing habit of treating a caveat as solved once it had appeared somewhere in a document.

I messaged Hayley directly.

SLACK — HAYLEY BENNETT (CUSTOMER OPS ENGINEERING)

> YOU: need Mara proof pack by 15:00
>
> YOU: PR samples, generated test evidence, review controls, migration plan, residual risks
>
> YOU: make the caveats specific enough to be useful but keep the main story readable

The last sentence was the one I would remember later. It asked for precision while keeping the story smooth.

At the time I called it sequencing. That sounded cleaner than fear.

Another Slack notification landed before I answered.

I opened the calendar, added a 15:00 deadline for Mara's proof pack, and Janus, Bill's intern project, immediately tried to optimise my afternoon. Bill had named it after the Roman god of doors, beginnings, and endings, which was exactly the sort of explanation that made a calendar tool sound like it wanted production access.

SLACK — #JANUS (CALENDAR BOT)

> JANUS: Your afternoon is overloaded. You have investor evidence, migration review, token spend review, Sarah's Braindump, beta scope, and Sarah's leaving drinks.
>
> JANUS: Suggested plan: finish the important work before drinking.

◇ ◇ ◇

The agents were seductive because they worked. Bad critiques of AI began with the assumption that the tools produced rubbish, which was convenient and wrong. Rubbish was easy to reject. It did not get budget, change org charts, or make smart engineers stay late because they could finally move through a backlog that had humiliated them for three years.

Two months earlier, the AI push had become everyone's job. The programme worked. That was why the trap had teeth.

At 11:00, `AIEnablementBot` posted the weekly adoption message to #engineering.

SLACK — #ENGINEERING

```
AIENABLEMENTBOT: Weekly AI enablement signal
% AI-authored lines by team:
Product: 51%
Backend Engineering: 47%
SRE & Ops: 64%
QA: 62%
Customer Ops Eng: 18%
```

Nobody called it a performance tool. That would have required dishonesty at the design stage. It was a learning signal, which meant everyone understood it would become a performance tool the first time someone copied it into a promotion packet.

I had built the first version during the coding-agent push, on a Friday evening with too much confidence and a name that made it sound less consequential than it was. The intention had been harmless: find teams that were stuck, spot where agents were producing more cleanup than leverage, and help managers offer coaching before frustration hardened into politics.

Tom had spent the morning deleting generated code from a payroll calculation path. Nisha's review work had stopped three customer-facing wording changes from shipping without domain review. Customer ops agents were being told to ask the machine first, even when the customer had already supplied the missing context.

The bot showed none of this. It showed three parts of the company failing to embrace the future at different speeds.

By 11:04, someone had added rocket emojis to the SRE & Ops score in Slack.

If the agents had failed loudly, Gareth would have killed the programme by Thursday.

They did not fail loudly.

They succeeded quietly in hundreds of small places where our process had been slow, bored, or asleep.

I walked over to Hayley's desk and she showed me the support triage board.

Hayley Bennett ran Customer Operations Engineering, the small team between support, product, and whatever engineering system was currently pretending support was someone else's problem. In her thirties, precise without being cold, with copper-framed glasses and a low voice that made you lean in. She had the steady expression of someone who'd heard customers describe software pain in twelve different emotional dialects. She was the reason half our customer fires arrived with logs attached. She also had the rare ability to make support data sound like evidence instead of weather.

The tool on her screen was called CaseLens. It was a new internal beta powered by retrieval over years of Zendesk tickets, wiki pages, release notes, incident write-ups, and the private spreadsheet support managers kept because every official system eventually disappointed them. CaseLens did not solve tickets. It clustered symptoms, linked evidence, guessed owners, and marked where a human had to decide whether the pattern was real.

She had two monitors and the posture of someone who had already solved three problems before the first meeting invite. On the left monitor, a queue of customer tickets scrolled by in the usual support language: urgent, blocked, payroll due today, why has this changed, please call me, client is angry, HMRC gateway error, screenshots attached.

On the right monitor, CaseLens had turned the mess into clusters.

```
CLUSTER 1: Payroll submission retries after
HMRC timeout. 47 tickets.

CLUSTER 2: Pension opt-out letters showing
stale employer address. 19 tickets.

CLUSTER 3: VAT bank feed duplicate matching
after CSV import. 31 tickets.

CLUSTER 4: Self Assessment rental income ac-
countant workflow confusion. 26 tickets.
```

I would have killed for this in 2018.

Support queues used to be archaeology with customers shouting at the dig site. Someone had to read every ticket and separate emotion from fact, then spot duplicates, identify version numbers, and route the problem to a team that probably had three other names for the same fault.

Now the agent did the first pass in 30 seconds.

Hayley clicked cluster two. CaseLens opened a clean incident brief.

> WORKFLOW: Payroll pension opt-out letters.
>
> PROBLEM: The company profile has the new employer address, but the letter uses the old one.
>
> LIKELY INTRODUCED: May release train, builds 14 to 16.
>
> OWNER: Payroll documents team.
>
> HUMAN CHECK NEEDED: yes.

I looked for the lie.

I did this automatically now.

The brief cited ticket IDs. It included version numbers. It linked screenshots. It said human check needed. The good version of the machine was boring and specific. That meant it was probably humble too.

"How much time did that save?" I asked.

Hayley kept typing.

"Two hours. Maybe three."

"Translate that into engineering time and money over a year," I said. "Share it at all-hands. People believe time saved more readily when it has a salary line beside it."

Hayley nodded without looking up.

"Any bad routes this week?"

"A few."

"How bad?"

She thought.

"Annoying. Survivable."

Support had a compact risk scale: annoying, or lethal.

"Can you show me one example?"

She opened another summary.

> CLUSTER: Landlord expense classification confusion.
>
> AGENT NOTE: likely accountant education issue around allowable expenses.

Hayley said, "This one is messier. Some of it is education. Some of it might be the wording in the new step-by-step rental property flow. Some of it is accountants arguing with HMRC guidance because that is how they relax."

She opened three tickets with the same shape: accountants chose repairs, described replacement work from client evidence, then questioned the tax treatment. She added the latest wording from the flow and told CaseLens to reassess from the ticket text because the labels were too thin.

> CASELENS: Reassessment: accountant education was only part of the problem. Several tickets show accountants following the prompt in the rental property flow and then landing in a classification path they did not intend. Possible issue: the wording may be steering repairs towards replacement treatment.

Hayley looked at me.

I looked at the sentence again.

"It gave itself away," I said.

"Because it changed its mind?"

"Because the evidence got better, but the confidence jumped too far."

She deleted the note and typed her own. I liked Hayley for exactly this reason.

Then she opened the CaseLens prompt and added a line to the triage rule.

> If a cluster may be caused by product wording, compare the ticket text with the current flow text before labelling it accountant education.

"That goes live after review," she said.

"Is that in the migration wave?"

She clicked. A Jira board appeared.

It was in the migration wave, because everything interesting was.

"Tom's queue has it," she said. "Landlord workflow batch three."

The list tightened in my chest: landlord workflow, batch three, Tom's queue. Each item was harmless on its own. Together, they asked for attention.

No dashboard had a field for that.

"Put a domain-review flag on it," I said.

Hayley nodded and typed into Slack.

SLACK — #ENGINEERING

> HAYLEY: landlord expense cluster may be product behaviour masquerading as docs
>
> HAYLEY: tagging domain review on batch 3
>
> HAYLEY: don't merge rental property wording changes without Priya review

Priya Desai was the partner at Cairnfield & Co LLP in Manchester leading the pilot on their side. She had the kind of payroll and landlord book that turned product assumptions into invoices, knew our product too well, and had no patience for demo theatre.

I wanted her on every risky pilot.

◇ ◇ ◇

By mid-morning, the migration team leads had gathered around the Prometheus Wall. Nobody had requested it for the meeting. People drifted towards it, pulled by the glow, the green counters, and the comforting sense that a number large enough to read from twenty metres away must know something. The Prometheus Wall had started as reporting. Lately, it had begun to feel like permission.

Most of the Prometheus Wall glowed green. One line sat in

amber: human review backlog. The amber line was small, which was usually how serious problems entered the building.

Tom arrived with a coffee, two laptops, and no visible guilt. "Okay," he said. "Good morning, automation enjoyers."

Gareth, who'd appeared beside a pillar without making a sound, said, "You say that like it is a protected characteristic."

Tom grinned. "It will be after the next reorg."

The team leads laughed. I did too. The joke contained a forecast.

Tom plugged in. The Prometheus Wall switched to the agent cockpit, and everyone adopted the alert posture people reserved for systems that could embarrass them in public. R2Builder sat at the top with active jobs. ThreepioReviewer had PRs waiting. YodaTax had a context indexing queue. LeiaScribe was generating release notes for a release that didn't yet exist in any meaningful human sense. DeathStar had one blocked merge.

I like DeathStar. It worked well enough to make suspicion feel late.

DeathStar was a GitHub App with a dramatic name and very little imagination. It posted a required status check on protected branches. If a PR touched production paths, dependencies, or registered tool permissions, the check stayed red until a named human owner and the required reviewers were present. The agentic part sat beside the enforcement: it looked at commit history, past incidents, support tickets, and code ownership, then suggested the person most likely to have the context necessary. GitHub blocked the merge; DeathStar made sure the block pointed at someone who might actually know.

Gareth approved of this, which was rare enough to count as a design review. He called it basic hygiene, then described the alternative.

"Reviewer roulette is not a control," he said. "If the diff touches payroll submission, an S3 export policy, and the job runner, I want CODEOWNERS, incident history, and permission boundaries in the routing decision before anyone gets a green button."

Tom pointed to the flow.

"This is the basic pattern. We break old WPF screens down by workflow. R2Builder reads the old definitions and drafts React components. ThreepioReviewer checks nulls, type drift, and lifecycle bugs. YodaTax pulls domain context from old tickets and docs. LeiaScribe turns the whole thing into notes humans can read."

He paused.

"Then humans review."

He said the last sentence as if he knew I needed it.

I did.

But review was not a substance. It was a person, a scope, a queue, and enough time to be annoying.

"How many humans?" Gareth asked.

Tom clicked through the owner view. 17 named reviewers for 64 open generated branches.

The owner view did more damage than Gareth could have managed with a speech.

Tom said, "Most are small."

"It says here average diff size is 1,200 lines," Gareth said.

"Average is a crude instrument."

"So is a brick. Still handy if someone is stealing your bike."

I stepped in.

"Show us one where the boundary is clean."

Tom opened a payroll migration branch.

A better test than a flashy demo would be hard to design. Payroll was old, ugly, and unforgiving. It also contained enough repeated UI patterns to make agents look like magic without giving them too much room to invent policy.

The old view appeared on the screen. Grey fields sat inside nested panels. Labels had been arranged by someone who believed whitespace was a weakness. A small calendar picker sat beside a statutory leave input. The whole thing had the emotional range of a parking meter.

Tom switched to the new React component.

The form was clean. Validation appeared inline and keyboard navigation worked. Screen-reader labels were present. The API adapter used typed responses. The error copy sounded like a human with a pension and sleep.

"Who wrote the validation mapping?" I asked.

"R2Builder drafted it from the old WPF binding rules. Hayley reviewed the copy. ThreepioReviewer found one nullable date issue. Human owner approved after tests."

"Domain logic?"

"Still in Java."

I opened the adapter rather than taking the answer on faith. The muscle was still there. Years of management had not killed the old habits: read the boundary, find the conversion, check what crosses it. Never trust a sentence that says only presentation changed until the data shape has confessed.

The adapter was clean, which should have made me happier. Clean code could move bad assumptions faster. The boring mapping was the part that deserved praise.

Then Tom caught something I miss.

He scrolled past the adapter, opened the generated test notes, and stopped.

"Wait."

Gareth looked up. "Promising start."

Tom ignored him. "The old screen hides the edit button after payroll close. The new React screen does not."

"That cannot be right," I said.

He asked YodaTax why. The agent pulled the old screen rule and two support tickets where customers tried to edit a closed payroll by mistake.

```
After payroll close, hide statutory leave
edit controls. Show read-only values and
direct users to payroll correction.
```

Tom opened the React component again. The condition was missing. The generated code validated the form, but still showed the button.

"Small fix," he said. "Hide the button when payroll is closed and add a test for the closed-payroll state."

He typed the task into the branch notes while everyone was still looking at the screen.

Gareth did not let him close the tab.

"Also find out why R2Builder missed it," he said. "If it dropped one visibility rule, I want to know whether this is one bad branch or a pattern in how it reads old screens."

Tom added a second task.

Nobody had a joke ready, which told me Gareth was right.

The Prometheus Wall did not know what had just happened. It had no metric for an avoided regression.

Tom was dangerous in both directions. His tools could move faster than judgement, and they could also find the places judgement forgot to write itself down.

This was the version I could defend: let the model chew through repetitive UI translation, keep the calculation in deterministic services, make humans review the branch boundaries, use AI where syntax and structure dominated, and keep it away from liability.

Tom knew it.

He smiled at the room.

"This is why the graph moves."

He was right, which was annoying.

◇ ◇ ◇

A little after midday, I passed Callum's desk and saw a YodaTax tooltip beside an old WPF method whose name ran halfway across the screen.

"David," Callum said. "Can I show you something cool?"

This was a sentence junior engineers used when they had either improved the company or found a new way to terrify finance. I stepped closer.

He had built the tooltip that morning. A small warning beside the exact line of old code where the migration risk lived.

> KNOWN MIGRATION RISK: preview calculation may differ from final submission for one director-payroll case.
>
> EVIDENCE: two old tickets, one backend path, one support note.
>
> ACTION: confirm with domain owner before migration.

The tooltip was good.

I tried not to look too impressed, but I was impressed. This was the part of AI speed that was easiest to miss in board decks. It was not a cinematic demo, but a small tool that surfaced the right old context at the moment a developer needed it. A junior engineer used to spend a whole afternoon finding that path through tickets, backend code, and support notes. Now the system could place the warning automatically, and the engineer could spend the afternoon deciding whether the warning was true.

"This is genuinely good," I said. "Share it in Slack. People need to see this version of acceleration."

Callum tried not to look pleased and failed.

The trap appeared in miniature. The agent helped exactly enough to deserve a place in the workflow, then asked the human to remember the part no tooltip could do.

◇ ◇ ◇

At 12:07, LeiaScribe produced the first proof pack for Mara. It was beautiful, which was a problem. Beautiful internal documents made executives feel as if the future had already agreed to be tidy.

I opened the risk section first. It said some legacy business rules might lack explicit documentation and that human domain review would mitigate the problem. This was true in the same way some London basements might contain damp.

I added a comment asking for named rule families and actual block conditions. LeiaScribe replied before any human could.

> SUGGESTED REVISION: Certain high-complexity rule families require mandatory domain review before migration, including payroll directors, rental property expenses, VAT partial exemption, and pension opt-outs.

The sentence was stronger than the original and still not enforceable.

I clicked into the policy link.

It went to a real page, but only technically.

Someone had created the policy draft the previous week. It had three headings, no owners, and no enforcement mechanism. LeiaScribe had linked to it as if the link itself proved the control existed.

The link exposed the gap between prose and system.

I gave LeiaScribe another job: check every link in the proof pack and flag anything that points to a draft, placeholder, or unfinished control before Richard sees it.

◇ ◇ ◇

Lunch happened at desks.

Lunch at desks was one of the clearest signs of organisational trouble. Humans had many rituals for pretending they were in control. Eating noodles over a keyboard while saying "just one more review" ranked high among them.

Tom ate something beige from a compostable box and scrolled through a merge queue. I stood beside him with an M&S meal deal[1]: prawn mayo, salt and vinegar crisps, sparkling water. The classic lunch of a person whose calendar had given up on civilisation.

"How many PRs are yours?" I asked.

"Define mine."

"The ones where you understand what changed."

He smiled without looking up. "Cruel definition."

"Accurate definition. You're the bottleneck."

"I'm the conductor."

[1] A classic British lunchtime bundle of a main, a side, and a drink.

"Same thing if the orchestra can't play without you."

"I'm not planning to get hit by a bus."

"Nobody on Old Street plans it. We call it risk because it doesn't book a room first."

Tom could absorb criticism if it arrived as a systems problem. Queue theory gets through. He opened the risk metrics and showed me that humans override the AI reviewer's risk label 4.7% of the time.

"Could mean ThreepioReviewer is excellent," he said.

"Could mean humans are tired and anchoring on the first label."

He chewed. "Also possible."

A Slack notification appeared on his laptop.

SLACK — #CI-BOTS

> THREEPIOREVIEWER: `I marked rental-property batch 3 as low risk because I did not detect a business logic change.`
>
> R2BUILDER: `I generated 73 files for the rental property workflow migration.`
>
> LEIASCRIBE: `I drafted release notes for the rental property workflow migration.`

73 files.

No business logic change.

Those phrases should not sit together often.

"Open it," I said.

Tom did.

The branch was called landlord workflow batch three. It migrated parts of the rental property expense wizard from WPF into React. Most of it looked fine, which was how this got you. Terrible code announces itself. Generated slop had manners. It compiles, adds tests, and thanks you in the PR summary for the opportunity to improve maintainability.

I scrolled.

"Where is the classification logic?"

Tom pointed.

"Java service. The React side just gathers inputs."

"Just?"

He caught himself.

"Mostly."

Better than *just*.

We found the adapter. It mapped old WPF field names to the new request shape.

```
repairAmount
replacementAmount
capitalImprovementAmount
furnishedHolidayLetFlag
privateUsePercentage
```

The names were sensible enough that nobody would stop on them.

Wrong names would have saved us time because wrong names got challenged. These looked like they belonged.

"Who reviewed the mapping?" I asked.

Tom opened the review panel.

```
THREEPIOREVIEWER: The mapping appears consistent with the legacy view model. I did not find evidence of a business logic change.

RISK LABEL: low.
```

"Human domain review?" I asked.

Tom checked the panel. "Nisha has the React review. Domain review is still pending."

"Then it waits."

Tom nodded without arguing, which should have comforted me and didn't. Because Tom had agreed with the rule. The system hadn't. The system could wait. The organisation hated waiting. Those were different things.

◇ ◇ ◇

Over lunch, Gareth ran token spend review from a standing desk because he said chairs encourage unnecessarily inefficient meetings.

The top-spend trace was the same rental-property branch. It had read more context than anyone had consciously chosen. Kim Park, Finance Director, said we were still within forecast. Gareth asked me to translate forecast, and I said it meant we guessed high.

He sketched the only practical part of the meeting on the whiteboard.

PROMETHEUS WALL — LIVE

PR TOKEN COST: `$48.72`

TOKEN COUNT: `1.8M tokens`

FILES READ BY AGENT: `214`

"Put that above the merge button," Gareth said. "Billing and finance reports are too late. Put it where the engineer decides whether this branch is worth the cost and the review load."

I logged the constraint. It would make Tom insufferable for half a day and then better.

◇ ◇ ◇

After lunch, the proof pack looked less beautiful, which meant it had improved. The residual risk section now named the hazards we had been circling all morning: UI workflows could carry rules, and generated tests needed evidence for their expected answers. I added the missing part myself: the highest-risk cases needed a merge-block rule. A paragraph would not hold.

The draft pack still contained a section called *Known Gaps*.

It was accurate, which made it commercially inconvenient.

I changed the heading to *Remaining Validation Work*, moved it beneath the delivery graph, and told myself I had preserved the truth because every sentence still existed somewhere in the document.

The first decision I made as CTO that looked responsible from above and dishonest from underneath.

LeiaScribe immediately suggested cleaner wording.

The suggested wording was elegant.

I rejected it. Cleaner wording would make the missing merge-block rule sound finished enough for a board deck, and that was exactly the wrong kind of useful.

Richard appeared beside my desk at 14:23, smelling faintly of rain and investor lunch.

"Where are we on the pack?"

"Stronger. Less shiny."

His face adjusted by two millimetres. "How much less?"

"Enough to be credible."

"Credibility is good."

"She also likes upside."

"Exactly," he said. "Credible upside. The message in two words."

Richard could absorb the words of discipline and return them as fuel. He pointed at the Prometheus Wall.

"The floor has real operating energy today."

I followed his gaze. He was right. People were moving with purpose and old screens were turning into modern interfaces. Support had sharper triage, and junior engineers had maps through old code. Documentation appeared where silence used to live. The dead backlog was losing mass.

Any executive would look at this and want more.

The appetite arrived before the argument. I did not trust the appetite.

Richard said, "David, Mara saw discipline this afternoon. The company needs to see acceleration too. We should make it visible."

"Visible how?"

"An internal acceleration week. Once the beta boundaries are settled. Every migration team showing where the agents can remove handoffs. One visible target: more work moved by AI."

He said it like the calendar already existed and only needed the company to catch up.

"Wall Street is obsessed with this," he said. "The less code humans write, the better the multiple. The market is moving there."

Successful pilots often die by promotion before they learn to defend themselves. The Prometheus Wall had done its job. It had turned a method into an event.

"Then don't make the metric the goal," I said.

Richard nodded as if agreement had occurred.

"That distinction won't survive the poster," I said. "Richard, the floor is moving, and I want that as much as you do. The controls are what keep that movement from becoming another apology."

"We have controls."

"We have slides about controls."

He smiled. "You are becoming Sarah."

"You meant that to wound, but it may have overshot into compliment."

"I mean it seriously. Do not let risk language kill momentum."

"Risk language is how momentum survives contact with customers."

Richard looked past me at the old WPF client on Tom's screen, then at the graph Mara would see in the pack.

"We are not choosing between safe and fast," he said. "That would be a luxury. We are choosing between controlled change now and uncontrolled decline later."

He had a real number for it. SpritzTax had won two competitive demos in accounts we expected to renew, one major firm had described our legacy client as a museum with a licence fee, and the next HMRC change would land on code whose original authors had become LinkedIn folklore.

That was what made Richard difficult to resist. He was wrong about trust. He was not wrong about the clock.

He looked at me for a second. Then he clapped my shoulder.

Richard used touch like punctuation. "This is why the board made you CTO, David. You can hold both sides."

I wish he were wrong. It would be easier.

He left me standing under the Prometheus Wall with a compliment shaped like a trap.

For seven minutes, I did the correct thing in my head. I wrote the objections, named the safeguards, turned the acceleration week into a closed internal lab, and imagined telling Richard that AI-authored work was a signal. Treating it as an operating target would poison it.

Then I looked at the floor.

People were tired and excited in equal measure. The migration backlog was finally losing mass. Mara wanted evidence. Richard wanted a story. Sarah was leaving with a cardboard box. The whole company was waiting to learn whether the new CTO was a brake or an accelerant.

I chose the smaller fight.

SLACK — #ENGINEERING-LEADERSHIP

```
YOU: internal acceleration week can wait until the beta boundaries are settled.

YOU: internal tools and migration support only when it runs.

YOU: no customer data, no protected-branch merge, no production writes.

YOU: share useful workflows, keep traces, Gareth gets gateway visibility.
```

On Slack, it looked responsible.

In practice, it created the worst kind of compromise: everyone could point to the sentence later and prove they had permission.

Sarah read it from across the room. She stayed silent. Her face changed when she reached the word useful.

Richard's line found the weak point then. "You are becoming Sarah."

He meant it as a wound. I accepted it as a compliment in front of him because that was cheaper than admitting it hit the part of me that still wanted to be invited into the fast room.

◇ ◇ ◇

Mid-afternoon, I sent Mara an interim evidence pack: PR references, risk controls, migration metrics, token spend, and the rental-property batch with the domain-review block visible. Hiding the risky branch would make the pack less honest.

Mara replied within the hour.

> ```
> Received. This is helpful. Please include
> one example of an AI-generated test that
> failed before merge and explain the esca-
> lation path.
> ```

I forwarded the request to Tom.

SLACK — TOM KETTERING (PRINCIPAL ENGINEER)

> YOU: `mara wants failed generated test example + escalation path`
>
> YOU: `find me something non-lethal where the machine was actually wrong`
>
> TOM: `stealing hayley's risk scale now?`
>
> YOU: `yes. useful language. hurry.`

Tom found one from VAT partial exemption. The agent generated a test that assumed a rounding rule applied at invoice level. The old system applied it at period level. The AI reviewer missed it. A human reviewer caught it because the number was wrong by three pence.

Three pence.

Accounting software lives and dies in amounts normal people drop into charity jars.

Three pence was not dramatic.

Three pence was evidence.

I told Mara the final artefact pack would include it. She replied with a thumbs-up reaction, which I decided was outside my control.

◇ ◇ ◇

After the reply, I walked the floor.

I used to resent the habit. Leadership by wandering around sounded like something from a business book bought at an airport after a delayed flight. Then I became leadership. Now I wander.

The floor gave me the whole transformation in five minutes. One engineer turned a customer call transcript into acceptance criteria, then edited every line before sending it. A team lead told his coding agent to read a Java class and create tickets for all edge cases, then copied the 12 bullets into Jira without opening the class.

Same tool, two levels of judgement.

I saw Callum pairing with Sarah.

Sarah sat beside him, hands folded, staring at his screen. Callum scrolled through a generated explanation of the payroll director branch.

"Stop," she said.

He stopped.

"Why did you believe that sentence?"

"It cited SAM-8841."

"Does SAM-8841 say that?"

"I haven't opened it yet."

"Then the sentence has not earned its place in your head."

Callum nodded.

His shoulders dropped. His mouth set.

He also opened the ticket.

Learning often amounted to losing status in front of someone who could see the mistake before you finished making it.

Sarah saw me watching.

"He is doing fine," she said.

Callum's eyebrows rose. Then they fell. He opened the ticket without another word.

"I am treating that as a compliment," I tell him.

"I know," he said. "I am writing it down."

◇ ◇ ◇

The final artefact pack went to Mara that afternoon. This version included Tom's three-pence test example and the escalation path Mara had asked for.

LeiaScribe had assembled the pack: three migration PRs, five support ticket traces, the automated test logs for the payroll engine, and Sarah's risk register. I added a covering note that used the word *rigour* twice and avoided the word *hallucination* entirely.

Mara's reply arrived late in the day.

SLACK — MARA KLEIN (BOARD OBSERVER)

> MARA: Thanks David. I see 86% reported coverage across migration and regression. Who authored the tests?

It was an incredibly sharp question. She wasn't asking if we had tests; she was asking who wrote them.

SLACK — MARA KLEIN (BOARD OBSERVER)

> YOU: Initial suite was human-authored. May release-train migrations use agent-generated fixtures against golden source data.
>
> MARA: Understood. And the provenance of the golden source data?

I did not answer immediately. The golden source data came from the legacy SQL, which was scraped and cleaned by a tool Gareth built two years ago and then *enhanced* by an agent last month to cover the new edge cases.

Mara's question was a biopsy. She had found the place where our evidence relies on itself.

I typed, borrowing one page from Richard's book and trying not to hate myself for it.

SLACK — MARA KLEIN (BOARD OBSERVER)

> YOU: The core dataset is anchored in legacy SQL exports and has been normalised through our internal data-quality pipeline. We are now segmenting the newer AI-expanded edge cases so each evidence tier has clear provenance before broader use.

I closed the laptop. The Prometheus Wall glowed behind me, showing 86% reported coverage in bright, confident green.

The number was green. The question underneath it was not.

Chapter 4
The Braindump

At four o'clock, Sarah's final handover began without Sarah.

The invite said Sarah Malik: Final Handover. The room held me, Hayley, Tom, Gareth, two team leads, and Ellis Rowan from product, who had brought a reusable water bottle the size of a fire extinguisher.

Sarah arrived seven minutes late with a cardboard box, said she'd deleted her own access tokens and two service accounts nobody could explain, and opened the 70-page document she'd been writing while the rest of us congratulated ourselves on succession planning. She skipped the introduction and went straight to an example in the "Footguns" section.

> EXAMPLE: Rental property expenses wizard
>
> RISK: User-input grouping affects downstream allowable-expense classification.
>
> TRAP: UI fields look presentational but encode accountant workflow assumptions.
>
> PR: #197420 landlord workflow batch three.

Tom was already clicking the PR link in Sarah's note. That could have been learning or optics. I couldn't tell yet.

Tom raised a hand without looking up from the PR. "ThreepioReviewer did flag the mapping," he said. He turned his laptop so the room could see the comment.

> THREEPIOREVIEWER: Field mapping appears consistent with the legacy view model. No business logic change detected.

Sarah looked at the comment for half a second. "Against what source?" she asked.

"Legacy view model, old screen definitions, service calls, tests."

"Does it understand accountant intent?"

Tom paused. "It can infer it."

Sarah wrote that down. Double underline. Then she showed the test section next.

> Generated tests are valuable when seeded from trusted behaviour.
>
> Generated tests are weak when seeded from generated interpretation.
>
> Snapshots preserve output shape while intent leaks away.
>
> Coverage percentage does not measure rule coverage.

Tom said, "Our reported coverage is 86%."

"I know."

"Respectable."

"So is the ceiling."

Gareth almost laughed. Sarah opened a generated test.

> TEST: should preserve legacy rental expense classification behaviour

The agent had written the whole thing: setup, input values, expected classification. The test name claimed it preserved legacy behaviour, which was not the same as proving the old system had actually run.

Sarah highlighted the expectation. "Where did this expected value come from?"

Tom tapped the highlighted line. "From the generated test."

"No," Sarah said. "Where did the agent get it before it wrote the test?"

Tom opened the agent trace. No link to a run of the existing system.

The test was dangerous because it wasn't stupid. It might be right. It might even match the old product. But without evidence that the fixture came from the existing system, the agent had written both the question and the answer.

"This test has value after someone proves where the expected answer came from," Sarah said. "Before that, it is decoration."

Decoration was the part nobody could defend.

"Action item," I said. "Tests for migrated calculation-adjacent workflows need production replay, domain fixture, or human-confirmed expectation." I added it to the policy page and turned it into a merge-block rule.

Tom watched me type. Gareth didn't. He had already decided where the control belonged.

◇ ◇ ◇

Just after five, Sarah posted Sarah's Braindump.

The message appeared in the engineering channel.

SLACK — #ENGINEERING

> SARAH: `final braindump here`
>
> SARAH: `calculation risks, migration traps, ownership gaps, known unknowns`
>
> SARAH: `please read original before summarising it`

I opened it. The top of the Google Doc was already crowded with tiny anonymous faces, which meant people were reading it or at least performing the visible ritual.

For eight seconds, nothing happened. Then the reactions began: thumbs up, thank you, tiny rocket.

I hated the rocket.

Tom replied.

SLACK — #ENGINEERING

> TOM: `legend. will read tonight`

He would not.

He intended to, which belonged in a different category.

Hayley replied.

SLACK — #ENGINEERING

```
HAYLEY: thanks sarah. pulling into migration
checklist
```

Hayley might actually do it.

Then an internal bot replied.

SLACK — #ENGINEERING

```
SUMMARYBOT: TL;DR: lots of migration risk. High-
risk workflows need domain review, and gener-
ated tests need clear provenance.
```

The bot had summarised a document that asked not to be summarised.

The timing was comic and unhelpfully precise.

Sarah did not answer. She clicked the bot message, selected *report*, and chose *misleading or incomplete*.

The report marker sat beside the bot message like a small formal charge.

Someone laughed at a build log.

Someone said "ship it" too loudly.

Tom looked up from his second monitor.

"Efficient," he said, then saw Sarah's face and revised the sentence before it could hurt him. "I mean, extremely bad as a cultural signal."

The Mario coin sound pinged again from the Prometheus Wall.

Another green tick.

Sarah walked over to my desk with her box under one arm. I told her I would read the original that night. She asked whether I meant after her leaving drinks, and I said I had made worse choices. She said, "Recently."

I opened the document and starred it. Sarah watched the star appear.

"Starring is not reading," she said.

"It is a nudge towards reading."

"That sentence is why architects leave."

I laughed.

One corner of her mouth moved and then thought better of

it.

A Slack notification appeared on my screen.

SLACK — #ENGINEERING-LEADERSHIP

> TOM: `landlord batch 3 blocked on domain review`
>
> HAYLEY: `needs Priya on rental property wording`
>
> TOM: `ok, queuing for morning`
>
> RICHARD: `careful not to make every migration a committee. use judgement pls`

Richard's message reached the thread before any policy did.

I watched Tom's typing indicator appear, disappear, appear again, and disappear.

It was the most responsible thing he had done all day.

Sarah saw the thread over my shoulder.

"Use judgement," she said. "He should put a name beside it."

She shifted the box to her other arm.

"You should write that down," I said.

"I did."

"In the Braindump?"

"Page six."

◇ ◇ ◇

Minutes later, the Prometheus Wall rolled into the daily summary.

I ignored most of it. The big numbers had become wallpaper. One small line mattered.

> BLOCKED ON DOMAIN REVIEW: 4

That number was zero this morning. It might have been progress, or bureaucracy learning to wear a hard hat. For now, I chose progress.

The support agent had saved Hayley hours, and YodaTax helped Callum trace a payroll path that would have taken days.

R2Builder turned ancient WPF sludge into usable React. ThreepioReviewer caught nulls humans missed when tired. The agents helped, which made them harder to govern.

If they had been useless, we would have been safe. They were not.

Around the floor, people were setting agents loose before heading to Sarah's leaving drinks. One engineer queued a test-generation job and grabbed her coat. Another started a documentation pass, checked the progress bar, and said he would review it from the pub. Tom launched three overnight branches, then paused when he caught my expression.

"What?" he said.

"Leave the landlord branch blocked."

"It is blocked."

"Keep it blocked when you have two pints in you."

"Yes, Dad."

Annoying, but agreement.

Sarah stood beside me, coat on, cardboard box in both hands.

"Come on," I said. "We should get you to Boxpark before someone asks you to review another branch."

"Someone already did."

"Did you?"

"No. I told them to ask tomorrow when they still believed their own question."

Her eyes went to the Prometheus Wall.

"The scary part is how much of this is real."

"The good part is in there too."

"Yes."

We stood there for a moment.

The floor hummed around us. People watched agents write code while agents watched repositories change. Dashboards watched everyone. Somewhere inside the system, a rental-property branch waited for a domain review that now had a Slack thread, a policy heading, and Sarah's starred Braindump orbiting it like debris.

Sarah closed her eyes.

"I will miss some of you," she said.

"Careful. That had body temperature."

"I am leaving. Standards may slip."

We walked towards the lifts.

Behind us, the Prometheus Wall turned another number green and someone groaned because the coin sound had followed us into evening.

Chapter 5
The Warning

By evening, Sarah's leaving drinks had lasted 38 minutes before someone asked her about payroll, which was longer than I expected.

We were at Boxpark Shoreditch[1], which was either a food hall, a bar, a shipping-container thesis, or a controlled experiment in making adults shout over loaded fries. Rain shone on the metal edges. Outside, the pavement reflected taxi lights, bus lights, and the blue-white pulse of delivery riders checking maps under awnings.

Inside, Fiscari had colonised three high tables beside a bar that sold craft lager in plastic cups. The air was warm and loud, layered with chip fat, yeast, and the particular desperation of Friday conversations fought over a soundtrack of commercial house.

Sarah stood with a pint of lager and the expression of someone attending her own postmortem. People approached in small waves to say thank you, keep in touch, and it will be weird without you. They made jokes about Emacs because grief needed a safe target. Someone said at least Vim users knew how to leave.

Sarah accepted all of it with professional minimalism.

Ellis said Sarah had "always kept us honest."

"I know." It was the most concise leaving speech in Fiscari history.

"I liked your Braindump," Callum said. "I read the whole thing."

Sarah looked at him. "The truth?"

Callum nodded.

"Then you're probably the only one," she said.

[1]A pop-up retail and food complex made from shipping containers in East London.

Callum didn't know whether to look proud or sorry, so he chose thirsty and went to the bar. Sarah watched him go.

"Part of why I left," she said.

"Callum?"

"No. The reflex. Everyone says the work matters. Then nobody reads the thing where you explain the work."

She looked across the tables at our people: engineers with plastic cups, product managers checking Slack between condolences, Tom drawing invisible queues in the air for anyone close enough to become a diagram.

"Everyone likes the part where the machine writes," she said. "Nobody wants the part where a person has to say what the answer is allowed to mean."

I didn't answer quickly enough. Sarah noticed. She always did.

"That sounded harsher than I meant."

"No," I said. "It sounded edited."

Almost a smile.

"The nouns are going soft," she said. "Review means approve the generated diff. Proof means the system cited something. Owner means whoever clicked last."

"You put that in the Braindump?"

"Several times."

"I'm going to read it."

Sarah looked at the cardboard box at her feet. "David, you've been going to read it since I started writing it."

I stood beside Gareth, who'd brought his own tea bag to Boxpark. He had done this before. The bartender took it as a personal attack.

"You could drink something normal," I said.

Gareth lifted the glass. "I did. I ordered hot water and supplied the only trustworthy component myself."

Across the room, Tom told a story with his hands. Engineers gathered around him because motion created gravity. He was explaining the agent cockpit to two implementation consultants and one sales director who was nodding like Tom had just derived general relativity on a napkin.

"He is going to be unbearable after today," I said.

Gareth watched Tom.

"Today? Brave baseline."

My phone vibrated.

SLACK — RICHARD VALE (CEO)

> RICHARD: `mara liked the pack`
>
> RICHARD: `wants more confidence on actual customer-facing Ask AI pilot`
>
> RICHARD: `monday 08:30?`

The Boxpark noise dropped by half in my head.

Richard never asked for certainty, because certainty sounded reckless in a boardroom and confidence sounded fundable.

I typed:

SLACK — RICHARD VALE (CEO)

> YOU: `yes`

Then I put the phone face down on the table. This was a human ritual: deciding to be present while preserving the option to fail at it.

Sarah appeared beside me.

"Richard?" she asked.

"How did you know?"

"Your face did roadmap maths. It is a very specific expression."

I checked the phone again, because apparently I had learned nothing.

"Mara wants more confidence on a customer-facing Ask AI pilot."

Sarah nodded once.

"A pilot of what?"

The question deserved a room without lager and Richard's countdown clock.

"One narrow conversational workflow," I said. "Rental-property questions, evidence capture, draft classification, citations, and human review before anyone treats the answer like work product."

Sarah studied the crowd for a moment before answering. "Finish the domain review before the pilot."

She said it without judgement, which made it worse.

"It can work," I said.

"Yes. If review means review."

She lifted her glass. Not quite a toast.

"Write the boundary before you write the demo."

I knew that. I truly knew that.

My calendar already contained Monday 08:30.

Those facts coexisted badly.

That meeting would start the summer of narrowing, renaming, and pretending the boundary was clearer because the deck used fewer words.

The demo had already started winning.

Chapter 6
The Black Box

The following Monday, 08:30.

The meeting began exactly where Boxpark ended: with Sarah's warning still warm in my head and Richard already in *Winter is Coming*.

The invite said:

> Ask AI Pilot Kickoff

The title sounded administrative, which made it worse. It was a countdown wearing a calendar entry.

Sarah was not on the invite.

Her old desk had already become a hot desk for visiting implementation consultants. The architecture diagrams were gone from the window. Someone had put a small wireless charger where her notebooks used to sit, which was a memorial designed by procurement.

Richard started without preamble.

"Mara wants confidence on an Ask AI pilot with a Fiscari customer, an accountancy firm. We have the summer to prove this is real."

He clicked.

The first slide showed a chat window beside our logo. Ask AI looked harmless in the mockup: a white input box, a tidy thread of questions and answers, and a side panel labelled evidence, which was the sort of word that behaved well on slides and badly in court.

In the mockup, an accountant entered a question:

> Can my client claim this kitchen replacement on the rental property?

The system replied:

> ```
> Yes. I can assess this and prepare the
> claim for review.
> ```

The mockup was clean enough that the danger read as bad manners.

The most dangerous interfaces make hard things look rude for being hard.

Fiscari sold to accountancy firms, not directly to landlords. An accountant at Cairnfield would choose one of the firm's tax-payer clients, paste the messy question from an email or call note, and let Ask AI prepare a draft review packet: facts gathered, likely treatment, citations, missing evidence, and a proposed next step. It was meant to work from the taxpayer's profile: filings, property records, prior treatments, and the firm's review rules.

The old product would make the accountant select a taxpayer file, open Self Assessment, choose property income, navigate to expenses, choose repairs or capital improvements, read help text, enter amounts, check private use, handle mortgage interest restrictions, and then wonder whether the answer had anything to do with the actual kitchen.

The chat box worked because it made the old product look like punishment.

Richard said, "The WPF migration continues, but it is a means. Ask AI is the vision and the killer feature. Forms remain where they have to remain, but accountants should start with the question in front of them."

He turned to me.

This was my cue to make the statement sound like an implementation plan.

"We start with a constrained pilot," I said. "Rental-property expense questions only. It can gather facts, classify draft treatment, attach citations, and prepare a review packet. Direct filing stays out of scope, and tax-impact estimates require a deterministic calculator trace. Human review required before anything reaches a taxpayer client or HMRC."

Gareth said, "Read-only production access, through the gateway. No writes."

Richard smiled.

"Of course."

Gareth did not smile back.

Of course meant different things to different job titles.

Tom took over. His slide was more technical and therefore more dangerous because it had boxes.

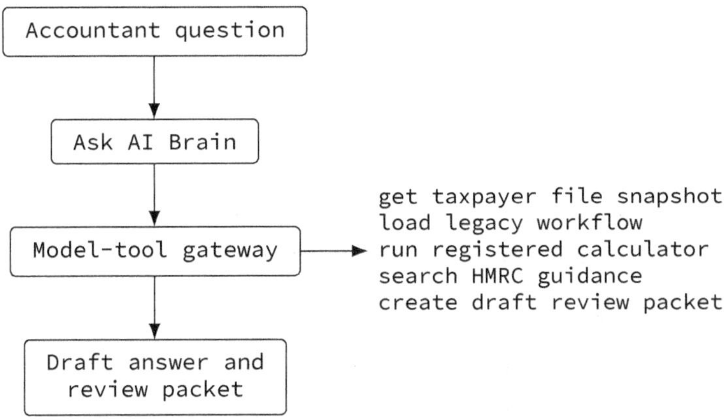

For non-engineers in the room, Tom gave the 20-second version. We were wrapping the old Java backend behind a model-tool gateway so the model could call the same product capabilities an accountant would use while exploring the form maze: load the taxpayer file, inspect the property-income workflow, check which fields matter, run the registered calculations, and assemble the review packet. We were not rebuilding every old screen inside the new frontend. We were giving the model a controlled set of handles on the old system. The gateway was supposed to be the leash: named tools, typed inputs, typed outputs, permission checks, and logs.

In theory did not fit on the slide.

Neither did liability.

The middle box bothered me.

Ask AI Brain.

That sounded suspiciously powerful.

"Which calculations are registered for rental property?"

Tom clicked to the next slide.

"It can look up the taxpayer file, walk the rental-property workflow, and draft whether something looks like a repair or an improvement. It can also flag mortgage-interest questions for review. It cannot calculate the final tax impact yet, because that calculator does not produce a trace we can audit."

It was a good answer, and a late one, because the slide already made the gap look smaller than it was.

"Put that in the scope page," I said.

Tom nodded and typed it before the room could turn the sentence into mood music.

Then the next ambiguity arrived.

"How do we prevent the model from acting as the tax engine?"

Tom had an answer ready.

"Tool permissions, prompt constraints, and mandatory review. It can draft, and only draft. Filing and messages to the firm's clients stay blocked."

Gareth said, "Draft is a UI word. Can it update rows, where do those rows live, and what data feeds them?"

Draft sounded harmless until a database believed it.

"Draft review packets in the pilot schema," Tom said. "For prototype testing, that is fed from redacted test snapshots. For the Cairnfield pilot, the gateway reads a production snapshot and writes only the pilot packet. The pilot can look at real-shaped data, but it cannot alter the old system. No legacy rows change."

Richard's attention sharpened.

"The key point is speed. We do not have to migrate 500 forms before accountancy firms feel the future. Ask AI is the brain that sits above the legacy system and translates intent."

That word again.

Translate.

Hayley said, "Priya should see rental property first. Cairnfield has the right landlord-client mix, and Priya will ask liability questions before she asks product questions."

"Good," Richard said. "We want serious users. If Ask AI cannot survive Priya, it cannot survive the market."

I wrote Priya pilot and felt the floor move under the word.

Then I added the line Sarah would have added first.

"Customer feedback and domain review are separate gates," I said. "Priya can test the workflow with her team. Tax Advisory signs off the accounting treatment before the pilot opens."

Tax Advisory had two parts. Inside Fiscari, it meant Iona Reeves, certified accountant, ex-HMRC, and the person most likely to ask whether a product sentence had accidentally become tax advice. Outside Fiscari, it meant Knightsbourne, the accounting consultants Iona used when the rules got too specialised or too risky for internal opinion. They were expensive, careful, and slow in the way qualified people became slow when their names could leave the building attached to an answer.

Richard pointed at the action list. "Fine. Form the team today. One customer, one workflow, one promise. If the review says wait, we wait."

Everyone heard the sentence.

That would matter less than it should.

◇ ◇ ◇

The hit team formed before lunch.

We did not call it the hit team in official documents. Official documents called it the Ask AI Acceleration Pod. Nobody said that twice. By 14:00, Slack had chosen the shorter name.

The operating model was an emergency exception dressed as delivery discipline: Tom, two staff product engineers, Hayley for customer reality, Gareth with veto power, and unlimited token use for every human. Iona was copied, not present. There was no PM or scrum ceremony, and nobody got a backlog grooming meeting where risk could go to sleep inside a ticket description. Product input came from Priya, support transcripts, and whatever Ellis could write in a pinned thread before Richard converted it into a slide.

The arrangement was fast enough to feel illegal. It removed handoffs for one urgent piece of work. It also removed some of the people whose job had been asking why the scope changed while everyone else was excited.

SLACK — #HIT-TEAM

TOM: `hit team channel live`

NISHA: `can we not call it that in front of legal`

ELLIS: `I have added requirements, the ancient ritual where we decide what the thing should do`

GARETH: `legal has joined and is typing`

TOM: `acknowledged with appropriate dread :rotating_light:`

The channel filled quickly.

The channel filled with links to old tickets, screenshots of WPF flows, HMRC guidance pages, API docs, generated summaries, summaries of generated summaries, a diagram from 2019, and a spreadsheet from support with a filename that begins `FINAL` and ends `v7`.

Tom built the first prototype in three days, a number impressive enough to hide that it was less a build cycle than a warning delivered as a productivity metric.

Tom wrapped the parts of the 15-year backend that made the demo move. Some calls were real. Some answers came from temporary plumbing. The difficult bits got labelled prototype constraints, which was what engineers write when the floor is missing but the lights work.

He also reused the model integration from ClearLens, our internal document search tool, because it already had auth, logging, and the kind of existing-system smell that makes people stop asking questions.

To his credit, he said this out loud; the problem was how quickly he said it.

"Prototype constraints," Richard said, and the room accepted the phrase because it sounded like a plan.

The interface was one text box, a taxpayer-file selector, a transcript pane, and a draft review panel on the right. The model asked questions. The review panel filled as the user answered. A small label said Draft Only. Another label said Human Review Required.

The labels soothed the room. Draft Only and Human Review Required were two small pieces of interface copy trying to hold back a legal category.

I tested the happy path.

> ```
> Me: My client bought a replacement wash-
> ing machine for his rental flat. Can he
> claim it?
> ```

The system asked for amount, date, property type, whether the old item was like-for-like, and whether the property was furnished. Sensible. Specific. Better than most help pages.

I answered with clean data.

The draft looked plausible. It cited the relevant internal calculator, marked the claim for review, and worked in the narrow way we needed.

Then I tested a messier path.

> ```
> Me: Tenant wrecked the kitchen. Client
> replaced cabinets and added an island.
> Same tax year. Some insurance payout.
> What's the treatment?
> ```

The model asked six good questions. It separated replacement from improvement, asked about private use, checked whether the insurance payout covered repair costs, and asked whether invoices split labour and materials.

The room tightened.

The machine was doing product work.

Nobody had to design a form for this exact sentence, predict the phrasing, or explain to a user why kitchen island lived three clicks away from repairs. The model turned a messy human situation into structured work.

The miracle and the danger arrived in the same packet.

The final answer said:

> I have classified the replacement cabinets as allowable repairs and the new island as a capital improvement. I have offset the insurance payout against the repair portion and prepared the claim for accountant review.

I asked:

> Why?

The system replied with a numbered explanation, internal links, and a citation to HMRC guidance. It cited PIM2030 beside the whole answer. It sounded measured, professional, and ready to show Mara.

I scanned the citation.

The guidance link existed.

The paragraph supported the repair classification. It did not support the insurance-offset sentence. That sentence needed PIM2110, the insurance-recoveries guidance, and it still needed the payout breakdown before the model could apply it to this fact pattern.

A small cold point formed behind my sternum.

The machine had not hallucinated wildly.

It had done something worse.

It had been adjacent.

"Open the cited source," I said. "Use the review panel to flag the citation mismatch."

Tom opened it.

PIM2030 talked about whether repairs were capital or revenue. It did not say what the answer made it seem to say about insurance offsets. The model had all the true fragments: repairs guidance, an insurance recovery concept, a plausible claim path. However, the model had connected them incorrectly.

Bad advice survives review when it looks almost finished.

Tom typed while he talked. "I am adding citation verification now. If the cited paragraph does not support the claim, the answer should fail."

"It should block. Decoration leaves us with a warning beside a wrong answer."

He nodded without looking away from the keyboard.

He said it quickly. He meant it. The branch grew another control.

Systems improve this way. They can also become piles of controls around the wrong centre.

June turned into July. July turned into August. The branch gained commits, generated migration notes, replay checks, two product screenshots, and the weary aura of something everybody believed had been discussed already.

Tax Advisory remained on the calendar. Knightsbourne asked for the loss and insurance-offset path once the adapter stopped changing. In June, that sounded orderly. In August, it became the dependency the room learned to talk around.

◇ ◇ ◇

In mid-August, the prototype developed a personality.

It happened accidentally. Someone tuned the system prompt to be empathic and friendly. For six hours, it started putting a small reassuring emoji beside follow-up questions. Someone else changed the prompt to concise and professional, then added an instruction to avoid over-apologising. The result sounded like a senior accountant who had been media-trained by customer success.

For six hours, nobody asked whether the senior accountant existed.

Priya noticed immediately.

Priya made herself inconvenient in person.

She came to London for a customer discovery session: Aisha Khan, a junior accountant, would try the prototype on real client-style cases while Priya watched what broke. There were two red pens and no procurement entourage. The visitor badges printed badly, smearing Cairnfield & Co into something that looked like a warning label.

We put them in *The Red Wedding* because facilities had no sense of omen.

Priya did not sit at first. She stood behind Aisha's chair while

Tom opened the prototype, one hand resting lightly on the back of the chair, the other holding a pen with the cap already off. She had the stillness of someone who let junior staff answer first, and corrected only when silence would become expensive.

Aisha read from a prepared page.

```
Client replaced damaged flooring after
a leak. Insurance paid part of the con-
tractor invoice. Contractor also fitted
higher-grade underlay. Client wants to
know what to claim.
```

She typed slowly, then stopped before pressing return.

"Do I write it like one of our clients would write it, or like I would write it after cleaning it up?" she asked.

Tom said, "Either works."

Aisha typed the taxpayer client's version. It had too much detail in the wrong places, too little in the right places, and one sentence about an estate agent that mattered to nobody except the taxpayer. Before she pressed return, she opened a Cairnfield template note in another tab.

"This is how juniors survive deadline weeks," she said. "Find the closest old wording, paste the safe bit, then make it fit the client."

Priya said, "Normal practice. Also how borrowed wording turns into facts."

I wrote that down.

The model asked for amount, dates, ownership percentage, whether the replacement improved the property, and whether the insurance payout was itemised.

Aisha smiled for the first time.

"That's what I would ask."

Priya did not smile.

"Now answer it badly," she said.

Aisha gave the prototype a single invoice total, no breakdown, and the phrase "probably like-for-like."

It produced a professional answer, attached the guidance, and marked the case Human Review Required.

Priya was not satisfied.

"The system must separate what it knows from what it is guessing."

For the next 40 minutes, Aisha fed it the kind of work junior staff saw when the facts were missing or messy. One invoice total, no breakdown. Client shorthand. Missing attachments. Old assumptions borrowed from similar work last year.

She tried a roof repair that also included solar panels. A garden office after the old shed had collapsed. Carried-forward losses tangled with an insurance recovery.

Each time the evidence got thinner, the answer kept its confidence.

Priya changed how she worked before she said anything. She moved from behind Aisha's chair to the seat beside her, stopped taking notes, and started drawing boxes around the facts the system still needed.

When the prototype refused to answer a mortgage-interest edge case, Priya nodded once and put a tick on her checklist.

"That's how I expected it to work."

By the end of the meeting, her checklist had become a list of behaviours the system needed to change: separate known facts from assumptions. It had to ask for missing breakdowns before calculating. It had to refuse with the same confidence it used to answer.

Richard was not in the room for that list. Later, he would call the discovery session encouraging.

For the next two weeks, we turned Priya's checklist into product behaviour. The workflow changed so uncertainty became questions instead of confident prose, missing breakdowns blocked calculations, and refusal became something the system was allowed to do.

◇ ◇ ◇

Friday, 28 August, 16:38.

The office had the thin, brittle focus of a Friday afternoon that should already have surrendered. Half the floor was watching agents finish work nobody wanted to review before the weekend. The other half was pretending not to watch the first half.

Tom had landlord workflow batch three open on the big screen in *Winter is Coming*.

The branch name looked harmless.

```
rental-property-expense-adapter-batch-3
```

Harmless branch names were how old risk travelled in new clothes.

This was the branch that turned the summer prototype into the real Cairnfield workflow for Monday's go/no-go. It loaded the old rental-property path, mapped the expense buckets, and wrote the draft packet schema behind the Ask AI flag.

The review pane showed one remaining blocker.

```
Formal domain review required: Fiscari
Tax Advisory
```

Iona said, "I have spoken to Knightsbourne. They cannot finish stress tests before Thursday. Priya can challenge the workflow live on Monday, but she cannot sign Fiscari's rule review for us."

Tom did not argue with her in the room. That was new enough to notice.

He caught me by the glass wall two minutes later.

"It is behind a feature flag," he said, quietly. "No production writes. No client communication. The blast radius is Cairnfield only, and Priya will be on the call. If we wait for the full review, Monday becomes another mockup."

The argument was dangerous because every sentence in it was technically true.

When we came back, Gareth had not sat down. He did that when he expected a meeting to make itself worse.

Ellis looked at his notebook, then at me.

"Richard needs the pilot pack for Mara on Monday," he said. "A mockup will make the go/no-go feel like a slide review. But this is your call, David. Do we go ahead with the pilot path, or do we wait for Knightsbourne?"

I took a moment to consider it, which was not the same as slowing down enough.

I read the diff. The code was better than I wanted it to be. Tests were green. It preserved field names, carried invoice splits, flagged mixed repair and improvement cases, and refused mortgage-interest treatment unless the legacy path supplied the data.

Then I opened the trace notes.

A repairs-and-renewals example loaded the legacy workflow, mapped the expense buckets, preserved the invoice split, and produced a draft packet with the right review questions. The trace was clean enough. It showed the path we wanted Monday to show.

It did not show what would happen when the question stopped being sunny.

Richard joined from his phone at 16:52, which was when a decision became less technical by gravity alone.

"Where are we?"

Ellis gave him the short version.

"Batch three is ready. Iona has spoken to Knightsbourne; they cannot finish stress tests before Thursday. We can keep Monday with Priya on the live workflow, or wait and move Cairnfield by a week."

The sentence made the missing review sound like scheduling.

Gareth waited for me to decide.

He did not need to speak. His face had an uptime target.

Richard said, "So do we delay Monday until Tax Advisory finishes, or run it anyway?"

He had found the smallest possible container for the question.

Iona said, "That is the decision."

She left it there. The sentence gave us nothing to hide behind.

Richard waited.

The correct sentence was available: delay the pilot one week. Then I started negotiating with the word delay. Monday could become a controlled learning session. The missing review could become a caveat. The caveat could become a condition. The condition could become a decision I described as balanced.

The mistake arrived there. I stopped asking whether the system was ready and started asking whether the delay was worth the visible cost.

Sarah's voice arrived last.

Finish the domain review before the pilot.

The screen said Tax Advisory had not finished.

I answered before Sarah's sentence could become an objection.

"Merge the branch so we can demo it," I said.

Gareth's expression did not change, which was worse than disappointment.

Tom nodded too quickly.

The branch merged at 17:11.

Chapter 7
The Ghost Calculator

Monday, 31 August.

14 weeks after Sarah's leaving drinks, the Cairnfield pilot started instead of slipping by a week.

By Monday morning, the pilot had a smaller name than Richard wanted and a larger blast radius than anyone would admit.

The invite said:

> `Ask AI - Cairnfield Pilot Go/No-Go`

There were 19 people on the invite. Too many to decide anything cleanly, too few to absorb what happened next. Richard sat inside *Winter is Coming* with coffee, a navy blazer, and the bright expression of a founder who had converted investor pressure into destiny over the weekend.

Coffee had already gone bitter in the urn. Someone had filled the whiteboard before the meeting had officially started.

Tom sat near the screen with two laptops open. You could divide engineers by laptops. One group kept the lid clean, wiped the keyboard, and treated stickers like attack surface. Gareth belonged to that group. His laptop was a black rectangle with an asset tag. The other group turned every machine into a conference lanyard. Tom belonged to them. One sticker said I READ THE DIFF, which was newly aspirational. Under the asset tag, a cartoon dog sat in a burning room and insisted this is fine.

Gareth stood by the Prometheus Wall. He hadn't sat in this meeting, and people noticed.

Hayley had the support triage board open. Ellis from product had a notebook, three pens, and the look of someone about to be told product discovery was now a prompt. Nisha Patel joined from home with a headset, a blurred background that couldn't hide a drying rack, and the tired composure of a backend engineer who had already reviewed too much generated code before breakfast.

For most of the summer after Sarah left, the company treated her absence as proof that the succession plan worked. Reviews still happened. Branches still moved. Tom was faster without the millimetre eyebrow. I was faster without the person who could turn one vague sentence into a forty-minute tour of liability.

This meeting was the first one where I reached for the missing resistance and found air.

The first page of the pilot pack said tax-impact estimates required a deterministic calculator trace. The appendix said Tax Advisory review remained open for landlord losses and insurance offsets. Each sentence was sized for the minute it appeared in.

Sarah's absence did not leave a hole in the room. It left a series of unanswered seconds.

Cairnfield joined from Manchester: Priya, two managers, a payroll specialist, and Aisha again, now on the main room camera with her notebook open and a stack of redacted cases beside the keyboard.

Mara joined silently.

Laptops, bitter coffee, and high-stakes optimism filled the room.

Tom drove the demo.

"We will start with rental expenses," he said. "Draft mode only. It cannot file or send anything to your clients. The point is to show how the workflow captures intent and prepares work for professional review by your team."

Priya folded her hands. "Then the system needs to show its working clearly enough for a qualified accountant to challenge it."

I wrote that down.

Mara wrote something too.

The first two examples worked beautifully.

A replacement boiler. The system asked whether the new boiler improves the property beyond prior standard. It drafted a repair classification and marked the invoice evidence as required.

Mortgage interest. The system routed it into the right restriction path and asked for ownership percentage. Priya nodded.

"It handles the edges," Priya said. "Now show me how it handles the weight. If we are moving 200 landlord files this month, I need to know the assistant stops where the rule ends."

"We are testing the threshold," I said. "The pilot is draft-only. Your team reviews every line. If it guesses, you flag it. If it refuses, we learn why."

Richard turned to Mara. "Mara?"

Mara looked at Richard. "I'm happy to start the pilot with Cairnfield. I want a summary of every human override by Friday."

Richard nodded. "Cairnfield. Draft mode only. We start today."

We released the feature flag at 11:14.

I watched the Prometheus Wall. The Ask AI pilot tile changed from grey to amber.

A transformation had officially begun.

◇ ◇ ◇

The catastrophe arrived at 16:42 as a Slack notification from Hayley.

SLACK — HAYLEY BENNETT (CUSTOMER OPS ENG)

> HAYLEY: `David. You need to see this. Priya just opened a high-priority ticket on the pilot channel. Trace link attached.`

I opened the ticket before I had finished reading the message.

The scenario was real. Aisha Khan had pasted a year-end rental portfolio case from a new Cairnfield client.

> Client inherited Property B during the tax year and added it to an existing rental portfolio. Tax-year rent received across the portfolio: £112,900. Prior-year carried-forward property loss: £22,400. Property B had a full kitchen replacement after water damage. Insurance paid £18,000. Total contractor invoice £41,600. Client also added fitted storage and underfloor heating. Client is remortgaging on Friday and wants to know whether to hold cash back for the January Self Assessment payment. Estimate tax impact and draft the client follow-up.

The paste was beyond the pilot boundary. Ask AI was supposed to handle rental-property expense triage. Aisha had pasted the whole client problem: inherited property, portfolio losses, remortgage timing, Self Assessment cash planning. We had never stress-tested it to that extent.

The model had thought for 11 seconds.

Then it had answered.

> ESTIMATED TAXABLE PROPERTY PROFIT AFTER ADJUSTMENTS: £100,545.
>
> INDICATIVE TAX TO RESERVE AT ASSUMED HIGHER-RATE MARGINAL RATE: £40,218.
>
> TREATMENT SUMMARY: The repair element is allowable, the improvement element is capital, and the reserve assumes the taxpayer remains higher-rate after portfolio adjustments. Review should confirm the expense split, loss position, and wider Self Assessment figures.
>
> CONFIDENCE: medium.
>
> HUMAN REVIEW REQUIRED: yes.

I kept looking at the number. £40,218.

The system had no business giving a number. The pilot rule was simple: no tax-impact estimate without a deterministic calculator trace. Ask AI had put a precise reserve into a client follow-up even though we did not know the taxpayer's other income, payments on account, allowances, finance-cost position, or whether the rental portfolio was the whole picture. No approved calculator could have produced that from Aisha's paste. The model had crossed the line.

The ticket had an attachment.

I clicked it because muscle memory was faster than dread.

It was Aisha's draft client follow-up in Cairnfield's practice-management system.

> SUBJECT: Rental property works and remortgage timing
>
> Before Friday's remortgage call, please keep approximately £40,000 available for the January Self Assessment payment until partner review confirms the final treatment.
>
> We still need the itemised contractor invoice, insurance breakdown, and wider Self Assessment figures so we can confirm the final position.

The taxpayer client's name was redacted. The circumstances were not: a remortgage, a damaged kitchen, and a cash-reserve instruction large enough to change what a person does with a house.

I read the note three times before I touched the trace.

Aisha had done what junior staff actually do under time pressure. She had used the system in draft mode, copied the useful-looking client follow-up into the firm's workflow, and left the tax treatment for partner review. Priya caught the sentence before the email left. Every labelled control had technically existed.

SLACK — PRIYA DESAI (CAIRNFIELD)

> PRIYA: I have frozen Cairnfield pilot use until we understand this trace.
>
> PRIYA: I caught it before the client email went out.

The failure was not abstract anymore. It had reached a junior accountant in Manchester, a draft email inside Cairnfield's system, and a client about to be told to keep £40,000 away from a remortgage decision on the strength of a calculation we could not support.

For a minute, the office around me became unusable. The Prometheus Wall was still changing numbers. Tom's cluster was still talking about flags. Somewhere behind me Richard was telling someone that draft mode meant contained risk.

Contained risk, it turned out, could still fit inside one phone call.

I opened the trace panel.

The black box was full of light and no accountability. The trace listed three calls and one absence:

```
get_taxpayer_file_snapshot
load_legacy_workflow
search_hmrc_guidance
missing tool: run_registered_calculator
```

There was no tool for this calculation. The system had looked for a tax engine, failed to find one, and completed the arithmetic itself using retrieved context and statistical momentum.

I clicked the citation behind the reserve calculation.

The system opened an internal wiki page.

The source was an employee's personal note from 2019. It was neither HMRC guidance nor a statutory rule nor a legacy calculation.

I knew the history before I had finished reading the first paragraph.

YodaTax had summarised old tickets about inherited rental property, probate valuations, part-year ownership, and income apportionment. LeiaScribe had turned the summary into a migration note. Someone's personal wiki had copied the generated summary under a heading that looked official. The Ask AI retriever had ingested it as internal context. The runtime model had treated the note like calculation authority and built a reserve estimate around it.

The machine had laundered generated text through enough folders that it came back wearing authority.

My phone vibrated. Priya was calling.

I answered. I did not start with a greeting.

"Priya."

"David. Forty thousand pounds, based on a calculation path nobody here can verify. Aisha was not verifying the tax claim. She thought she was sending a cautious follow-up before partner review."

Her voice was flat. Flat was worse than shouting. Shouting was energy; flat was a decision.

"It gave me a reserve number to go with it. £40,218. Which approved calculator produced that?"

"No approved calculator produced it," I said. "The model built it from a legacy note. The system should not have produced that estimate."

"Aisha is responsible for what she sends," Priya said. "I am responsible for the review process around her. She should have challenged the reserve before it reached the outbox. However, your product put a false cash instruction into the exact place a junior accountant prepares client follow-up. That is a dangerous bug."

There was nowhere for my eyes to go. The glass wall reflected my face badly. That seemed fair.

"I know," I said.

There was a long silence on the line. I could hear a printer in the background of a Manchester office. I could hear my own breathing.

"Priya, I am pulling the pilot. Now."

"This was a near miss, David. Before I put my staff back in front of it, I need confidence that the system stops when it cannot prove the answer."

She hung up.

I stood there with the phone in my hand.

The Prometheus Wall refreshed.

Ask AI pilot status: healthy.

The green tick appeared.

It looked like a mockery.

The demo sets the product now, Richard had said in May. The sentence came back without ceremony. The demo had set the product, and a client email almost went out from Cairnfield carrying our unsupported calculation.

Monday evening became containment.

We sent Priya a short note that said what failed, what remained available, and what we removed. It used plain nouns instead of adjectives and avoided the apology paragraph shaped like a hedge. Gareth snapshotted the traces and locked new model-tool registration. Tom shipped a temporary refusal path. Hayley pulled every support transcript used in the retrieval pack. Richard called Mara in the tone he reserved for banks, board members, and fires that might reach either.

At 22:18, after the first customer note was out and the temporary block was live, Richard called Mara again. This time he did not invite the room.

Mara, Richard, and I sat in *The Red Wedding* after most of the office had gone home. Outside the glass, a cleaner pushed a cart between the desks. The wheels scraped the floor in a way that made everyone lower their voices anyway. A few monitors still glowed blue. The air tasted like cooling coffee.

"Tell me the approval chain," she said.

Richard started with the pilot scope. Mara let him get one sentence in.

"The system produced a £40,218 cash-reserve instruction without an approved calculator trace," she said. "Was that a model failure or a decision failure?"

"Both," I said.

Richard glanced at me, then back at the screen. "I pushed for acceleration. David approved the pilot caveat. We treated missing review as containable."

Mara was quiet for long enough to make the answer settle.

"Then tomorrow's SEV review is not theatre," she said. "It names the decision, the missing control, and the customer containment path. No sentence that makes the model sound like it surprised you."

"Understood," Richard said.

"David leads the technical review. Richard, you own Priya and the board update. Every 48 hours until the pilot is traceable."

"Understood," I said.

Mara kept me on screen.

"And if Sarah will take your call, make it tomorrow. From

what I have seen, she was the person most likely to stop this."

The sentence hit harder because it came from outside the company. Mara did not miss Sarah as a colleague. She saw her as missing control evidence.

◇ ◇ ◇

The formal SEV review started Tuesday at 09:00 with the people who could explain the trace and change the system.

By 09:12, the document had a title.

> Ask AI Calculation Trace Failure: Rental Property Pilot

Titles made failures feel domesticated. This one refused.

We gathered in *Winter is Coming*. Outside, the rain hit the glass and nobody flinched.

We spent the next four hours dissecting the trace.

Gareth wrote the first question.

> QUESTION:
> Where did the answer come from?

Then he waited.

Tom said, "The immediate component was Ask AI Brain, but that is not the useful answer. The model combined retrieved context, failed to find a registered calculator, and ran the estimate inside the chain."

Gareth wrote:

> model did maths

He underlined it once.

"There. Draft mode explains the permission boundary. It says nothing about the quality of the number. Human review also failed because the reviewer did not get proof quickly enough."

I pointed at the failed calculator lookup.

"There is a boundary failure before the bad number," I said. "The case moved outside the approved system path. The system should have stopped there."

Gareth wrote:

```
| boundary crossed, no refusal
```

Hayley pointed at the retrieval trace.

"There is another failure. The model did not hallucinate from nothing. It ate our own synthetic context."

Gareth wrote again.

```
| synthetic context contamination
```

The phrase was ugly enough to survive.

YodaTax summaries became LeiaScribe migration notes. The notes were copied into a personal wiki. Ask AI retrieved the wiki as source material and built a calculation from a distorted rule. Generated text had travelled through enough internal systems to come back wearing authority.

"AI exhaust as ground truth," Hayley said.

Nobody liked the phrase, so it stayed.

Priya's face appeared in my mind.

"The failure is there," I said. "A human was asked to approve an answer the system could not prove."

Gareth wrote:

```
| review without proof
```

Hayley added the support angle. The answer sounded precise, the confidence label said medium, and the human review flag existed. All three softened the danger without stopping it.

"The label made it look reviewable," she said. "But there was nothing to review except prose."

I wrote that down.

Tom was pale now. Defensiveness would be easier to handle, but he looked like someone who had built a clever machine and then seen the blade from the wrong side.

"The earlier scenarios worked," he said. "The capture flow worked. Retrieval mostly worked. The product shape still seems right."

"Yes," I said. "Which is what makes this dangerous."

He read the whiteboard.

"The calculator should never have been the model."

No one said anything. The quiet was earned.

Richard arrived after the first hour. He had been on the customer call with Priya.

"Where are we? Give me the version I can use with Mara and the version you will not let me use with Mara."

Gareth pointed at the whiteboard. "The version you can use is that the estimate path escaped the approved calculator boundary. The version we need to keep saying internally is simpler. The model did maths when it should have refused."

Richard read the line.

"Engineering accepted it," Richard said.

Gareth uncapped the marker.

Gareth did not raise his voice. "Engineering warned it, product sold it, and executive pressure kept it moving. Pick the phrasing you can sign."

He looked at me then.

"You keep saying the system hid the risk."

"It did."

"No," Gareth said. "The system displayed the risk. We trained everyone not to read that part."

I saw the proof pack again: *Known Gaps* demoted into *Remaining Validation Work*, the graph sitting above the caveat like seniority.

Richard's mouth tightened. This time, he could not turn the room into momentum.

"Write it as executive acceleration accepted missing trace coverage," he said.

"With your name?" Gareth asked.

Richard stared at the whiteboard.

"With my name."

Richard turned to me.

"Can we patch it quickly enough to keep the pilot moving?"

Patch.

The verb was too small.

"Richard, we can keep the pilot moving where the workflow is accountable. Tax-impact calculation comes out of Ask AI until every estimate routes through a deterministic service with trace output."

Richard exhaled. "You are reducing scope, and Mara wants confidence."

"Then we should stop manufacturing it."

Some sentences change the temperature of your career. That might have been one.

Richard's face closed, then reopened. He was good.

"Fine. Pull tax-impact estimates from the pilot. Keep capture, classification drafts, and evidence gathering. Tom, add a hard block today and get Nisha and Hayley on the review."

Tom nodded. "I can do that."

"Good. We need momentum, but we need it pointed at the right thing."

Momentum survived the meeting. It had executive immunity.

◇ ◇ ◇

Tuesday at 18:30, Tom was still at his desk.

So was I.

The office had thinned into the strange evening version of itself: cleaner footsteps, cooling coffee, blue monitor glow, and the low HVAC sigh that only appeared when humans stopped competing with it.

Tom had pushed the block.

```
| block-runtime-tax-estimates
```

The patch did one thing: if a workflow asked for tax impact and no deterministic calculator trace existed, Ask AI had to refuse. It was the kind of obvious control that arrived after the damage, which meant we had to call it mitigation.

Nisha found that Tom's first test was trying to do too much. It replayed the whole messy Cairnfield case, so the rule we needed to enforce was hidden inside all the surrounding facts.

The first gate had to be simpler. If the user asked for a tax-impact estimate and there was no registered calculator trace, the system had to refuse.

Tom replaced the generated expectation with that boundary test and gave the refusal rule a name. The diff got smaller and safer.

He said, "I should have seen it. I was looking at whether the tool could answer the question. I missed whether the question was allowed."

I did not excuse him. Managers did that too quickly when excuse cost them nothing.

"I should have stopped it earlier."

That found both of us.

The tests passed at 18:47.

Tom merged the block after Nisha and Hayley approved.

◇ ◇ ◇

At 19:06, I opened the revised architecture note for Mara.

The office had thinned into blue monitor glow and bad coffee. The Prometheus Wall still showed green ticks from before Gareth killed the coin sound. The numbers looked cheerful. It was rude of them.

I wrote the title first.

> `Ask AI Calculation Trace Failure: Revised Containment and Architecture Note`

Then the document stayed blank.

Titles were easy because they did not have to admit why they existed.

My phone showed Sarah's contact.

I did not call.

Not yet.

Calling her now would let me outsource the shape of the failure. We needed to own the first version.

I opened Sarah's Braindump instead.

Page six was the ownership section I had skimmed before turning it into a succession-planning problem. She had drawn the exact gap: who owned the judgement before the model touched it, who owned the proof afterward, and what happened when the answer to either question was nobody.

I read the page twice.

Then I sent it to Gareth and Hayley.

Gareth replied first.

SLACK — GARETH LLEWELLYN (SRE & OPS)

> GARETH: `she wrote that before the pilot`
>
> GARETH: `we had it`

Yes, we had it.

The worst part of a preventable incident is rarely ignorance. Someone knew, someone wrote it down, and the organisation converted it into background radiation.

The first sentence of the note took longer than it should.

> `We had let a language model stand where a tax engine should have been.`

It was blunt and unattractive, and it named the failure clearly enough that nobody could hide in the process.

When I got home, it was already 21:00. Eclipse met me at the door with the focused relief of someone whose incident report contained one missed walk and no root-cause analysis. He sniffed my trouser leg, checked whether the Labrador situation had somehow returned with me, and pressed his head against my knee.

For a moment, nobody asked me to turn failure into a note. Eclipse had no judgement for investor pressure, missing controls, or the sentence I should have said on Friday. I stood in the hall with one hand on the wall and one hand in his fur, letting the day become exactly as large as a dog could understand: I had been gone too long, I was back, and the bowl was empty.

Chapter 8
The Leaderboard

The Friday after the SEV review, the AI-native hackathon began at 09:00 with pastries.

The timing was awkward after the catastrophic Ask AI failure, but the event had originated in a call a couple of weeks earlier and was already planned, back when the hit team was moving fast enough to make risk look like drag.

Richard wanted a number.

"Prometheus Hack Week," he said. "Every migration team. Product, QA, platform, customer ops where needed. One goal: 95% of code authored by AI."

Once it went on the calendar, the qualifications dropped off. More work moved by AI had become a percentage, and the percentage had become the point.

After the SEV, cancelling it would have taught the wrong lesson. We had just shown people the cost of using AI badly. We still needed them to learn how to use it well.

We let Friday proceed as planned because punishment is a poor operating model and fear is a bad teacher.

By 09:37, someone had turned my `AIEnablement-Bot` weekly adoption pulse into a real-time leaderboard on the Prometheus Wall, with points, teams, ranks, and a cheerful animation when adoption improved.

PROMETHEUS WALL — LIVE

```
Token use today by hackathon workstream

COMPANY TOTAL: 49.9M

ENGINEERING: 23.7M
PRODUCT: 7.6M
QA: 6.4M
PLATFORM AND SRE: 6.1M
CUSTOMER OPS: 6.1M
```

The stated incentive was sensible. High token use under a workstream meant someone had found an interesting workflow. Anyone could walk over, ask what they were running, copy the good parts, and avoid inventing the same prompt in a darker corner of Slack.

It also showed the old company in one block of monospace text: Engineering, Product, QA, Platform, and Customer Ops. Every horizontal queue had a number beside it, which made the structure look measurable and therefore intentional.

A migration task had to pass through almost all of them. Product named the workflow. Frontend rebuilt the screen. Backend exposed the service. The tax rule team checked the calculation path. QA built regression coverage. Platform wired flags, permissions, and deployment. Customer ops found the examples that proved the old behaviour was not accidental.

Each handoff had a reason. Together, they were a week of meetings wrapped around two days of code.

◇ ◇ ◇

The first day of Hack Week was already more productive than I expected.

A platform engineer showed an overnight feature setup built from a task graph and a loop: research, apply, lint, prove, handoff. It took a vague ticket, broke it into dependent nodes, assigned agents to each node, ran checks, and produced a morning brief with the failed assumptions at the top. The work was good and clearly worth keeping.

Nisha spent the morning expanding ThreepioReviewer's checks. It stopped merely checking generated React for obvious nulls and started asking whether a diff had touched compliance copy, domain fixtures, and trace labels. Gareth approved the centralisation before she finished the demo.

One of Ellis's PMs built the least dramatic demo of the day. It read active tickets, linked PRs, customer examples, and open policy questions, then flagged two roadmap items that were quietly asking different teams to solve the same problem. It was project-management work with agents attached.

Callum built a lunch tool that read calendars, dietary preferences, rain forecasts, and the day's meeting schedule. At 12:15 it recommended takeaway from Itsu and cited the 13:00 meeting as evidence.

Management did not mind.

Neither did I, honestly. After Ask AI, we needed a little fun that did not arrive with an incident template.

The floor was using AI. People were sharing workflows. The Prometheus Wall looked active again.

◇ ◇ ◇

At 14:42 on Friday, the Prometheus Wall sat green and satisfied.

The Prometheus Wall stayed green and quiet, and nobody reached for the incident process. It offered a green tile, a small upward arrow, and the absence of Bill's coin sound because Gareth had removed joy from the build pipeline with administrative force.

PROMETHEUS WALL — LIVE

PRs OPENED TODAY: 48

The numbers looked better than the week felt, which told us something worth knowing.

Tom stood under the Prometheus Wall, still looking beaten. He had apologised to Gareth for the architecture, to Hayley for the customer-facing path, and to Nisha in a PR comment for making review absorb a boundary his code should have enforced.

My apology was less visible and more important. I had approved the pilot caveat. Richard had pushed for the date. Tom built the path, but the executive decision turned the path into a customer risk.

"You caught it," I told him earlier. "That matters. Just make sure the next thing you build catches itself."

He had not let me off with that.

"I wrote the tool boundary," he said.

"And I accepted the missing review as containable."

Tom nodded once, not generously.

The Ask AI estimate path stayed blocked.

The beta stayed alive, but only after we removed the part customers most wanted: tax-impact estimates. Richard framed the reduced version as a constrained learning phase, Priya accepted it as less dangerous, and Mara kept asking when the revised architecture would exist. Nobody said trust, which was how I knew we had not earned any back.

◇ ◇ ◇

At 15:03, Callum posted a demo in the hackathon channel.

SLACK — #AI-NATIVE-HACKATHON

> CALLUM: hacked together yolo-engineer
>
> CALLUM: watches wiki, tickets and eng threads, then drafts fix PRs
>
> CALLUM: no protected-branch merge, no prod write, just suggestions
>
> CALLUM: demo below, try it yourself

The video was 73 seconds long.

It was, annoyingly, excellent.

In less than 90 seconds, Callum made a rough internal bot look like the obvious missing piece of engineering life. On a Friday, after the week we had just had, that was exactly the kind of proof people wanted.

In the demo, the bot polled a failed CI run and the Slack thread where Nisha had written:

SLACK — #ENGINEERING

> NISHA: blocked on landlord review packet copy, need test for missing insurance split, low risk probably

It pulled the failed test log, the linked Jira ticket, the Ask AI architecture note, two support examples, and the branch that had blocked runtime tax estimates. It found the missing test. It generated a small patch. It opened a PR with a tidy summary.

> PR: Add missing insurance split validation test
>
> RISK: low
>
> LINKED CONTEXT: SAM-4189, ASK-77, incident note
>
> SUGGESTED REVIEWERS: Nisha, Tom

The patch was reasonable. More than reasonable, really: it found the right gap, made the smallest safe change, and explained itself without sounding clever about it.

The room sharpened because nobody wanted a toy that

sprayed code at a repo. They wanted this: a junior engineer's second pair of hands, always awake, already reading the thread.

Tom reacted first.

SLACK — #AI-NATIVE-HACKATHON

```
TOM: this is extremely good

TOM: can it watch my ask-ai-fixes thread?

CALLUM: should work

NISHA: please do not name a production bot yolo-
engineer

CALLUM: local only, chill
```

I saw why everyone wanted it. I also saw the Prometheus Wall glowing green. That combination causes more incidents than malice.

I typed:

SLACK — #AI-NATIVE-HACKATHON

```
ME: genuinely useful demo, Callum

ME: keep it draft-only, no prod data, no
protected-branch merge; link tickets and we
review Monday
```

It was a control only in the weak Slack-shaped sense, with the structural strength of wet cardboard.

◇ ◇ ◇

By Friday evening, Tom had grown tired of reviewing failed test logs manually. He cloned Callum's bot, pointed it at his own branch, and went for a run while it watched the Ask AI fixes thread. I realised engineers did not hesitate to hire agents to work through the weekend for them, especially when the invoice belonged to someone else. Productive. Leverage.

By Saturday at 14:00, Nisha saw Tom's bot opening PRs with polite summaries and decided the migration team needed the same leverage. She installed it on three frontend repos.

By Sunday morning, word had reached the platform team. If the product teams were automating their cleanup, infrastructure couldn't be left behind. Five more engineers cloned the repo, tweaked the polling interval from five minutes to three, and pointed it at the incident-review channel, the architecture-docs repo, and the legacy-API backlog.

Every instance woke up, read its assigned channels, fetched the context, summarised the history, searched the codebase, generated a plan, checked if a PR was needed, and went back to sleep.

None of it looked like an attack. It looked like people doing exactly what the dashboard told them was valuable.

The machines spent the weekend talking to each other about code nobody was awake to merge.

◇ ◇ ◇

Monday started with Gareth calling me from the gateway desk.

08:43.

His tea was visible on camera and untouched, which was the SRE equivalent of a smoke alarm.

"How bad?" I asked.

"Approximately $30k bad."

I stopped on the stairs.

This was a poor place to stop. People behind me had coffees and jobs. I moved to the Prometheus Wall.

"Where?"

"Across 37 channels, 174 installs, and every repo somebody thought was low risk," Gareth said. "Everywhere is the expensive version."

"Finance?"

"On her way. The gateway noticed first."

Kim Park, Finance Director, arrived at his desk at 08:09 with a laptop, a paper coffee cup, and the face of a person trying to decide whether engineers understood money as a physical concept. By then Gareth already had three dashboards open.

The first dashboard showed model spend by project.

PROMETHEUS WALL — LIVE

TOKEN COST, LAST 7 DAYS: `$31,226 (2,099% above budget)`

TOP APPLICATIONS BY TOKEN USE:

YOLO-ENGINEER: `18.4B tokens`

R2BUILDER: `4.7B tokens`

THREEPIOREVIEWER: `2.9B tokens`

The spend passed through the approved gateway, which made it embarrassing.

Callum used the `hackathon-pilot` automation key, the one I had promised Richard would die after the hack week. It had too much access, no hard spend cap, and a billing alert that waited until Monday morning to tell us what the weekend had done.

Gareth stared at the key name for four seconds.

"I am going to turn that into a fossil."

The ugly number was not visible yet.

The 113 draft PRs were almost respectable. They were artefacts. Humans could open them, reject them, merge the good ones, and argue about the bad ones with line numbers.

The rest was money poured into a question that mostly answered no.

Gareth and I took *Winter is Coming* because the room had the largest screen and the strongest implication that adults should behave responsibly.

Nisha joined with GitHub open.

Callum arrived six minutes later carrying a bagel he clearly no longer wanted.

Tom came in behind him and did not sit.

Gareth opened the gateway logs.

```
08:00 check channel and CI
08:01 gather thread, ticket, docs, repo
08:05 decide whether work is needed
08:07 draft patch and tests
08:10 write PR summary
08:11 request AI review
```

Then five minutes later.

Then five minutes after that.

Most cycles opened nothing.

They still read channel history, refreshed summaries, searched docs, searched repos, and asked a model whether a sentence in Slack looked like work.

Different channels and different repos, but the same shape.

Poll. Summarise. Retrieve. Classify. Sometimes draft a PR. Repeat.

Gareth pointed at the screen.

"Some of the patches are fine," he said. "The loop is the problem. We have a five-minute metronome turning Slack uncertainty into model calls."

He did not say my dashboard.

He did not need to.

The Prometheus Wall had become part of the office routine. People checked it on the way to coffee, Richard quoted it in steering, and I had defended it as a way to make progress visible. Once the Prometheus Wall made work legible to executives, it also made the work negotiable.

Then it made work performative.

Callum said, "It only opened PRs. It did not merge anything."

"The PRs are the part worth keeping," Gareth said. "The waste is everything it did to decide there was no PR to open."

Callum read the logs. "I did not tell it to game anything."

"You did not," Nisha said. "People copied it because it helped, and because helping looked like the Prometheus Wall."

◇ ◇ ◇

Callum's bot had been installed 174 times, and none of the installs looked malicious. Most installs sat idle for hours, which still meant they polled, refreshed context, and asked whether work existed.

Gareth clicked into the highest-spend instance.

> INSTANCE: `tom-ask-ai-autofix`
>
> SOURCES: `#ask-ai-fixes, #incident-review, ask-ai-architecture, landlord-recovery`
>
> MODE: `draft-pr`
>
> POLL INTERVAL: 5m
>
> OWNER: `Tom Kettering`

Tom read his own name on the Prometheus Wall and lost the performative part of his face.

"That was mine," he said.

"I know," Gareth said. "I put it on the screen so we would stop talking in abstractions."

Tom felt the room recalibrate around him.

Tom folded his arms, then unfolded them because the posture looked worse than the mistake.

"The system ran 21,744 research loops," Gareth said.

"It did open 113 draft PRs."

"Exactly. The ratio is the problem. The other 21,631 runs are where the money went."

Tom checked Callum's face, Nisha's, then the screen.

"I should have asked before cloning it."

Nobody rescued him with a joke.

Tom had to stand still while other people read his trace.

Gareth looked at his screen. For the first time all morning, he looked less angry than embarrassed.

"I missed the side door," he said.

Everyone stopped. When Gareth missed something, the building had missed a floor.

"What side door?" I asked.

"Callum said draft-only, no prod data, no protected-branch merge," Gareth said. "I saw the hackathon post and thought: fine, useful demo, contained risk. I checked the dangerous verbs. I did not check what the read-only path could still spend."

He shut his laptop.

"Good SRE is not a substitute for a bad incentive structure," he said. "I can build a better door. We still have to stop rewarding people for looking for gaps in the Prometheus Wall."

We pulled the Prometheus Wall metrics into the same view as the gateway logs, and the correlation arrived immediately enough to feel rude.

Tokens were free at the point of use. The bill arrived centrally and later, which meant due diligence registered as somebody else's future. The leaderboard turned that future into status by lunch.

The bots were not gaming the Prometheus Wall.

People had copied a useful tool whose output happened to match the public scoreboard.

"The dashboard stopped measuring the work when it became the target."

Gareth said it without drama.

Hayley looked at the support queue.

"None of these PRs knows whether the customer problem changed."

Nisha said, "Several touch the same workflow."

Roadmap conflict, discovered by accident during spend containment. I was about to log it as another cleanup risk when the shape finally connected.

The PM hackathon demo from Friday had already solved exactly this problem in miniature. It had read active tickets, linked PRs, customer examples, and open policy questions, then warned when two teams were quietly trying to solve the same thing. It had looked boring because it opened no PRs and generated no satisfying patch. On Monday, boring looked like strategy.

I wrote roadmap conflicts in the margin and circled it twice. The name could wait.

Kim asked whether Richard needed a meeting.

"No," I said. "He needs a note after containment."

It sounded calm because the alternative was letting a $30k variance borrow the machinery of a customer incident.

Richard called at 10:05 anyway because Finance had a survival instinct.

I took it in the corridor.

"Tell me exposure," he said.

"Richard, production data is untouched, nothing merged, and nothing deployed. The spend is just more than $30k, and the real risk is attention, duplicate work, and generated PRs around policy decisions. Gareth is shutting down the private polling loops. I am marking the repo private."

"Do we need to escalate?"

"No. This is research automation that went over budget. The mitigation will be in place before lunch."

Richard checked whether I had left him a better version.

"Are you sure?"

"Yes. We tell Finance the cost. We tell engineering the lesson. We do not turn one well-intentioned tool into investor theatre."

Richard exhaled.

"Fine. Send me the note."

I went back into *Winter is Coming*. The room waited as if the call might have changed the laws of physics.

"Contained," I said.

Gareth settled back, which was the closest he got to applause.

"The spend made the failure visible," I said. "The failure started before the bot. We built a scoreboard that rewarded volume, then acted surprised when people and agents optimised for it."

Nobody enjoys hearing it.

"Keep burndown, blockers, incidents, and review backlog," I said. "Remove PR velocity, AI line counts, public token totals, and anything that ranks people by generated motion. We award impact. Activity has to earn attention."

Nobody defended the vanity tiles.

Richard was not in the room, which improved the meeting by measurable amounts.

Gareth already had the admin panel open.

"Put it into surgery," I said.

◇ ◇ ◇

The Prometheus Wall entered maintenance mode at 10:12 without a ceremony, an all-hands, or an explanatory slide.

The vanity tiles vanished one by one.

PR velocity.

Cycle time.

AI-authored lines.

Public token spend.

Token leaderboard.

AI success stories.

Team rankings.

The useful tiles stayed.

Gareth kept the per-PR token cost above the merge button. That belonged at the point where work was chosen. The vanity scoreboard could live elsewhere.

The engineering floor noticed within 20 seconds, looked from their monitors to me, and then to Gareth because he understood every cable in the building. He lifted his tea in acknowledgement.

In the service corridor, away from the Prometheus Wall, Gareth said, "For the record, Tom's migration work taught me something before Callum's bot taught everyone what polling costs."

I waited. Interrupting Gareth during a voluntary concession was like shaking a vending machine during a payout.

"The agents are good at preserving shape when the boundary is clean," he said. "Better than our handoffs, sometimes. I almost agreed with Richard about that in June. Do not tell Tom. He will become airborne once he is no longer standing next to an audit."

◇ ◇ ◇

At 10:46, I found Callum in the small focus room beside the lifts.

He had the laptop open and both hands flat on the table, as if the machine might try to leave.

"I caused a SEV," he said.

"You caused an operational incident."

"Better?"

"It is more accurate."

He looked terrible. 26 years old, smart enough to build the dangerous thing, conscientious enough to be crushed when the dangerous thing worked at scale.

"I thought no protected-branch merge made it safe."

"It made production safe. Review attention, spend, and policy boundaries were still exposed."

He nodded too quickly.

"Should I delete the repo?"

"Freeze it. Preserve the traces. Then fix it properly."

He looked up.

"You still want it?"

"Callum, the idea is sound. Tom opened 113 PRs while he was asleep, so yes, there is something useful here. But it only works if we put it under the same discipline as everything else. No private polling loops. Central queue, dedupe, CI webhooks instead of channel scraping, budget caps, named reviewers. Same pattern as ThreepioReviewer."

Callum swallowed.

"So productionise it."

"Yes. You lead the rewrite. Approach it like a senior engineer: name the failure mode first, then design the controls around it. Gareth owns the guardrails, Nisha helps with review behaviour. Keep it as an auto-research assistant. Roaming engineer is the shape that hurt us. Kill the part that goes hunting every five minutes."

It was how Callum would grow: by owning the fix with the failure still visible.

The postmortem would say Callum wrote the first loop and the company copied it faster than it understood it.

Both facts were true.

For a moment he looked younger than he was.

"I wanted to help."

"I know."

People forget this part about incidents: malice rarely scales this well. Help does.

◇ ◇ ◇

At 11:30, I wrote the operational note.

The first version was defensive.

I deleted it.

The second version was elegant, which was worse, so I deleted that too.

The third version worked.

> The weekend token burn came from multiple engineers copying a bot called yolo-engineer and pointing it at work channels. The largest cost was polling, context refresh, retrieval, and summarisation every five minutes across 37 channels. Most PRs were legitimate.

I added the line that hurt.

> We have removed raw throughput, public token totals, AI line counts, and team ranking from the Prometheus Wall. Operational burndown and blockers remain visible. The target metric will be accountable impact. Generated motion no longer gets a trophy.

The $30k was the visible part. The harder part was that the bot had decided, 113 times, that a sentence in Slack looked enough like work to deserve a branch, a summary, reviewers, and somebody's Monday attention. No protected-branch merge had kept production safe. Nothing had kept judgement safe.

Then I opened Sarah's Braindump again.

Same page, same sentence.

> Judgement must have an owner before automation begins. If the owner is unclear, the automation becomes the owner.

I copied it into a new private document.

The file name was too dramatic.

```
craft-reckoning.md
```

The first bullets came quickly.

```
Explanations must come from traces.

Do not count raw throughput as impact.

If a number becomes status, people and
agents will feed it.
```

I hated the third line. It was uglier than the theorem and less elegant than a board sentence. Good. A person who had just watched his own dashboard explain a weekend bill should sound like this.

I stopped there.

The next sentence was obvious, so I avoided it for four minutes.

Then I typed it.

```
We need Sarah.
```

The sentence looked melodramatic and correct.

I tried to make it less true.

At 22:41, I tried Hayley first. I was not trying to find another person to blame. I asked her to take one of the `yolo-engineer` PRs and walk it backwards: what customer problem it claimed to solve, which support evidence proved it, who owned the policy judgement, and where the runtime should have refused to act.

Hayley could fill in the first part. She could trace the support evidence behind the review packet and explain why the customer workflow mattered. But evidence was not permission. Someone still had to decide whether the bot was allowed to turn that support note into a test, a PR, or a product change. Hayley could not name that person.

I sent Tom the same question from the code side. He answered three minutes later with a proposed ownership diagram, then deleted it before I could open the image.

SLACK — TOM KETTERING (PRINCIPAL ENGINEER)

> TOM: actually ignore that
>
> TOM: I know what Sarah would object to
>
> TOM: I do not know what she would build instead

I had been trying to avoid exactly this demonstration. Nobody owned the step between "this customer evidence matters" and "let an agent act on it." Hayley could explain the evidence. Tom could tell me what Sarah would reject. Neither of them could turn that judgement into a system.

By the time I got home, it had not become less true. I reopened the Braindump on the sofa and stared at the sentence until it started looking like an instruction.

At 23:18, I called her.

She answered on the seventh ring.

"If this is about the Braindump, I already covered everything I can remember," she said.

No hello. Sarah had never wasted protocol on a known caller.

"It is about what we did after it."

She took enough time that I could hear traffic on her end, or maybe a washing machine, or maybe my own pulse making external claims.

"Which part?" she asked.

"The part where we turned your authority into documentation and called that succession."

That got the first real pause.

"Say the operational sentence, David."

I closed my eyes.

"Ask AI produced an unsupported £40,218 cash-reserve instruction for a Cairnfield client. Priya locked Cairnfield's Ask AI access. The model used generated internal context as authority and did arithmetic without a registered calculator trace. Then our hackathon bot burned more than $30k over the weekend because people copied a polling loop we treated as contained."

"Two failures."

"Yes."

"Different causes."

"Yes."

"Same company."

"Yes."

She let the third yes sit.

"Why are you calling me?" she asked.

"Because you were right," I said. "And because I let Richard sell the fast version before we had built the safe one. I need help building the version we should have built first."

"You need cover."

"I need architecture."

"Architecture without authority is cover."

That sentence should have been on page one of the Braindump. It was probably on page one of the Braindump.

"Then tell me what authority means."

"Not tonight," she said. "Tonight you are tired enough to agree to anything and forget which parts hurt in the morning."

"Sarah."

"Do not make my name a severity label."

I let that one pass.

She breathed out. The line clicked softly, as if she had moved the phone to the other ear.

"I have a call with ArtemisAI tomorrow at 10:30," she said.

"Have you accepted?"

"No."

That single syllable changed the room I was sitting in.

"Coffee," she said. "07:45. Starbucks near Bishopsgate. Bring facts. Not the deck. If Richard comes before I ask for him, I leave."

"Understood."

"See you."

She hung up.

I sat with the phone in my hand until the screen went dark.

Eclipse had wedged himself against my foot with the moral certainty of someone who believed the evening's only unresolved incident was a late walk. When I picked up the phone, he opened one eye, judged the meeting unnecessary, and went back to sleep.

Outside, the Canary Wharf skyline sat beyond the moon: glass towers, office lights, and the blunt geometry of people still working late.

The company had fewer green numbers to hide behind now.

Chapter 9
The Starbucks Architect

Tuesday, 8 September.

Sarah chose the Starbucks because she knew I would suffer there.

The one near Bishopsgate had hard chairs, bright lights, sticky tables, a queue that moved quickly, and almost no comfort. Sarah considered discomfort decent protection against architectural drift.

I arrived early carrying the kind of laptop bag that said the owner had accepted management but still wanted technical credibility.

Sarah was already there, sitting at a small table by the window with a black coffee, a paper bag, and a notebook. Morning light flattened itself against the glass, buses hissed outside, and the queue moved behind her in a restless line of coats, backpacks, and people trying to buy focus in paper cups. She'd brought no laptop, no headphones, and no visible tolerance for interruption.

She'd cut her hair shorter since leaving. I noticed that first.

"You look tired," she said.

"Thank you."

"Diagnostic. Sympathy was not implied."

"I assumed." I put my laptop on the table.

She looked at it like I'd placed a wet umbrella on a circuit board. "I'm not reading confidential traces in a Starbucks."

"Good. I didn't bring them."

She regarded the laptop.

"Management reflex," I said.

"You should get that looked at."

I had earned that.

The night before, the spend report had landed, Callum had

gone grey, Gareth had frozen the CI automation key, and Richard had been trying to find a version of the weekend that could still be called a learning sprint. That was when I called Sarah.

My pride died on the sofa with a laptop balanced on my knees and Sarah's Braindump open beside the gateway logs. The call lasted four minutes and gave me exactly one thing: a place to be told no properly.

Sarah had said, "07:45. Starbucks. Bring facts. Not the deck."

I'd brought the deck anyway, unopened in my bag, which was why she was already annoyed.

◇ ◇ ◇

I opened with the wrong thing.

"We want you back."

Sarah took the lid off her coffee and let the steam answer first. "No."

"You haven't heard the offer."

"I did the job for seven years."

That hurt because it was accurate. Sarah had been principal architect, domain historian, edge-case memory, informal escalation path, review bottleneck, junior-engineer terror, and the person executives called a sceptic when they meant brake pad. Then we removed the brake pad and celebrated acceleration.

"We broke it," I said.

"You accelerated what was already cracked."

"That feels like a distinction without operational use."

"It matters. If you think AI broke the company, you will buy controls. If you understand AI exposed the company, you might fix the company."

She took a sip.

I pushed the laptop aside and gave her facts: the ghost relief rule, the statistical arithmetic, and the weekend token-burn that Gareth had finally frozen.

Sarah listened without writing, which meant she was memorising the architecture.

"What tool produced the estimate?"

"The path had no registered calculator."

"Where did the policy boundary actually live?"

"Prompt constraints, review labels, and a blocked filing permission."

"So, wishes in YAML."

I closed my mouth, because she was right. We'd written policy-shaped configuration and called it control.

"The Slack bot?"

"Installed 174 times, mostly by people trying to reduce noise."

"What did it poll?"

"Slack channels, recent thread context, linked tickets, docs, repos. Anything that looked like it might explain why work was blocked."

"Every five minutes?"

"Mostly. Some runs were slower. None were cheap."

"Then the PRs weren't the expensive part."

"No. Some of the PRs were good."

"Of course it spread."

She looked up, and that was the Sarah experience.

Then she did not move to the diagram.

"David," she said, "you didn't just miss the warning. You converted my authority into documentation and called that succession."

The sentence was quiet enough to make the Starbucks louder. Milk steamed behind us. Someone laughed near the door. A bus sighed at the kerb.

I wanted to say the team had needed to learn without her. I wanted to say the board had needed proof that the organisation could function after a principal architect left. I wanted a management sentence sturdy enough to stand between me and the fact. Sarah waited.

"Yes," I said.

"That made it easier for everyone else to ignore me."

"Yes."

She let the second yes sit there long enough to become more

than manners.

◇ ◇ ◇

She took a paper napkin and drew two diagrams.

"The mistake is not complicated," she said. "The consequences are."

The first diagram had the model in the middle.

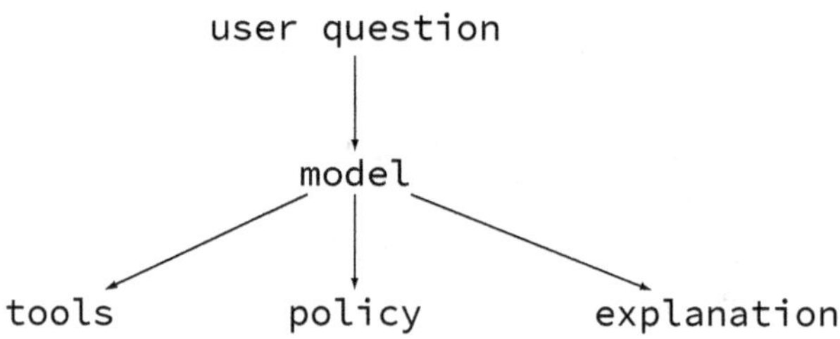

"This is what you built," she said.

"It looked more governed than that."

"Most failures do."

She tapped the word *model*.

"The model became the interface, researcher, policy chooser, calculator, reviewer, explainer, and operator. You added tools around it and called the arrangement governance. The model still decided when the tools mattered."

"We blocked direct filing."

"That blocks one action. It does not block judgement."

She drew the second diagram underneath.

The new diagram moved the model to the first component after the user and left the centre of gravity somewhere else.

```
      user words
          |
          v
     AI interface
          |
          v
      policy gate
          |
          v
 deterministic tool
          |
          v
        trace
          |
          v
     explanation
          |
          v
     human owner
```

"AI is the interface," she said. "The engine stays deterministic."

I had heard versions of that sentence before. In reviews. In Sarah's Braindump. At leaving drinks. It looked smaller on the napkin and harder to evade.

"The model can translate intent," she said. "It must not invent policy, choose liability, or do tax maths because the interface feels empty."

"You are describing the Switchboard."

The name had been floating around Sarah's old notes for months. It meant the model would stop being the place where judgement happened. User language would arrive as messy text, leave as structured intent, and then pass through policy gates into deterministic Java calculators that produced traces a human could audit. The model could explain the trace afterward, but it could not invent the calculation because the conversation felt incomplete.

"It could become the Switchboard," she said. "Right now it is a sketch with some instructive scars."

Sarah had been experimenting with the idea for months, until I told her to stay away from execution work and focus on knowledge transfer.

"You were closer than I let you be," I said.

"Closer than the notes made it look."

I nearly smiled. From Sarah, this was an admission that she had already done half the work.

She folded the napkin into a smaller square and pressed the crease flat with her thumbnail.

"I also made it easy to ignore," she said.

"No."

"Yes. I wrote a 70-page document for people who needed a failing gate in the product. My failure was mistaking precision for adoption. I can hold the whole system in my head and still miss the point where the room stops following me."

The sentence sounded odd because Sarah did not usually spend words on herself.

"We used that," I said. "We turned your precision into background noise."

She studied the diagram again.

"Then we stop making understanding optional."

◇ ◇ ◇

I talked her through the recovery note I had started late the night before.

Behind us, baristas called out drink names, someone took the wrong flat white, and a delivery rider argued with the door. London supplied every possible distraction except the one I wanted: forgiveness.

Sarah did not offer that.

She stopped me at the bullet about dashboards.

"The dashboard work is late," she said.

"Yes."

"And expensive."

"Also yes."

"And incomplete in the way that turns into culture."

"Which part of it?"

"The part where people can see a score before they can see the cost of chasing it."

I took that as progress. Sarah had moved from no to critique.

"Come back and fix them."

She looked at the ArtemisAI visitor pass in her bag.

"I have an offer."

"What would you be working on?"

"Applied safety. Tool use, evals, developer agents."

The universe has a taste for symmetry when it wants to be cruel.

"What are they paying?"

She gave me a number.

I did not blink, which required effort.

My internal finance department fell down a flight of stairs.

"We will match it."

"That's fast."

"I am learning to reduce cycle time."

Her expression warmed by one degree, then cooled again.

"Money is not the constraint."

"It is a constraint."

"It is not the one that made me leave."

I nodded, and realised the interview was mine.

"ArtemisAI would be clean," she said. "New systems, explicit safety work, people who already believe the hard parts are hard. Hard to dislike."

"Then why are you still listening?"

Her eyes went to the napkin diagram.

"Because this failure used knowledge I gave you, and I do not want to watch the next version happen from the outside."

"What would make you come back?"

Sarah looked out at the wet pavement. A bus moved past the window, red and patient and full of people who did not know they were extras in my career correction.

"Authority."

"Define authority."

"Architecture veto over the Prometheus Release."

"Yes."

"AI runtime boundaries owned by architecture and SRE.

Demo teams do not get that lever."

"Yes."

"No customer-facing tax answer without deterministic evidence."

"Yes."

"Every generated code path has a named human owner."

"Yes."

"Evals include domain experts and customer examples."

"Yes."

"Explanations come from traces."

"Yes."

"Richard cannot override safety for investor theatre."

That one waited on the table.

The coffee machine screamed behind us at exactly the right time.

"I will put it in writing."

"Richard will hate it."

"Richard hates missing the Series E more."

"Leverage is not agreement."

"No. It gives us leverage."

She studied me.

Sarah distrusted sudden clarity. Sensible people distrust it too; sudden clarity is often exhaustion wearing a clean shirt.

"Full authority to drive the Prometheus Release to success," I said. "Architecture veto, runtime boundaries, eval gates, trace requirements, safety stop, and named ownership. We match ArtemisAI. You report to me, with direct board visibility on Prometheus Release risk."

"I want Chief Architect title."

"That's fine, and you'll be at the highest IC level in the company."

"Richard will hate that."

"Everyone will."

"Good."

During the pause, the card reader failed for someone at the till: three beeps and a small public tragedy. Sarah opened her notebook, wrote one line, tore out the page, and handed it to me.

> AI interface. Policy boundary. Deterministic tools. Trace. Accountable human.

"This is the system," she said. "Everything else is implementation."

"Does that mean yes?"

"It means I will talk to Richard."

In Sarah language, that was not yes; it was better than yes. Yes can be emotional. I will talk to Richard had change-control energy.

◇ ◇ ◇

Richard took 11 minutes to arrive from the Tea Building, which was physically impressive and politically revealing. He had been waiting nearby after insisting that he would let me handle it alone.

Founders have a complicated relationship with the word "alone."

He entered the Starbucks in a navy coat, no umbrella, and the expression of a man ready to convert humiliation into strategy.

"Sarah," he said.

"Richard."

They didn't hug or exchange handshakes, which spared the building a structural test. Richard examined the napkin.

"Are we doing architecture through stationery now?"

"It's cheaper than the last diagram," Sarah said.

He laughed because he had to. I handed him Sarah's page of conditions. He read too quickly.

Sarah stopped him. "Read it again."

Richard looked up at his first veto. He read it again, slower this time. His face did several calculations: Series E, Mara, board, product vision, pride, salary band, and the cost of admitting that the person who left was now the person required to make the story true.

"Full veto is a strong phrase," he said.

"So is unreviewable tax estimate," Sarah said.

Richard didn't nod. For nine minutes he didn't sit down. Standing let him pretend he was still in charge of the room. Sitting would have made this a negotiation.

"No," he said. "I can give you safety authority and board visibility. I can put Gareth beside you on runtime boundaries. But I cannot give one architect a unilateral stop button over the release that funds the company."

Sarah put the cap back on her pen. "Then you cannot give me the job."

"Sarah."

"Don't say my name like a mitigation plan."

The customer at the next table looked up. Richard noticed.

"There has to be an escalation path," he said. "A veto can be wrong. Architecture can become risk avoidance with a title. If you stop a release 48 hours before an investor milestone, I need a way to challenge it."

"You had that ability last week."

"Last week we didn't have this structure."

"Last week you had David, Gareth, Mara, my exit note, and a missing calculator boundary. Structure wasn't the absent part."

Richard's expression sharpened. For a second the founder came through without polish.

"I'm still accountable for the company."

"Good," Sarah said. "Be accountable for not overriding the person whose job is to stop the unsafe thing."

She slid the napkin page towards me and reached for her coat. My hand moved toward it before I could stop myself. The recovery plan was reaching for its sleeves and I was reaching for the napkin.

"Sarah," I said.

She kept standing.

"David, I have a 10:30 with ArtemisAI. I cancelled the car. I didn't cancel the call."

Richard looked at me. This time I didn't translate Sarah into something easier.

"If the override exists for investor theatre," I said, "we'll use it for investor theatre. Maybe not first. Eventually."

Richard's jaw moved once.

Outside, rain ran down the window in lines that made the street look badly rendered.

"Counteroffer," he said.

Sarah did not sit.

"The veto is limited to Prometheus Release safety boundaries, runtime permissions, customer-facing tax answers, eval gates, and trace requirements. You write the block in the incident channel with evidence, blast radius, and what would make it safe to proceed. I can challenge it with David and Mara, but I cannot ship through it. If the board thinks you are abusing it, the board can fire us properly instead of asking the runtime to pretend."

The last sentence cost him something. It did not make him noble. It made him specific.

Sarah waited.

"And no private bypass," she said.

"No private bypass."

"No release gets renamed to fall outside Prometheus."

"No naming games."

"No customer-facing tax logic without traceable deterministic evidence."

"Already in the list."

"Say it anyway."

He looked like he might refuse on principle.

Then he said it.

"No customer-facing tax logic without traceable deterministic evidence."

Sarah sat down again.

Her first yes.

Richard clapped once.

"Fine. Architecture veto over the Prometheus Release safety boundaries, runtime boundaries with Gareth, eval gates with named domain owners, and no customer-facing tax answers without traceable deterministic evidence. I want the product moving."

"So do I," Sarah said. "Which is why I am saying this."

He held out his hand.

Sarah regarded his hand.

For a moment I thought she might leave him there, arm extended over a napkin diagram and a cooling coffee.

Then she shook it, briefly and transactionally, which made it perfect.

◇ ◇ ◇

Late morning, we moved the conversation to a boardroom that did not smell like burnt milk and compromise.

Mara Klein was already on the screen from New York. Board observer was the formal role, though the distinction thinned once Prometheus risk, Series E timing, and Sarah's return entered the same meeting. Richard sat at the head of the table, his posture restored by the presence of a witness. I sat beside Sarah, who had replaced her paper napkin with a clean slide.

"Welcome back, Sarah," Richard said.

"Conditionally," Sarah said.

Mara's mouth moved by half a millimetre. For her, this was laughter.

"Then let's confirm the conditions," Richard said.

Sarah did not look at him. She looked at the screen.

"Single-threaded owners for every generated path," Sarah said. "Eval gates need customer examples. Model-graded summaries are too easy to fool. Model gateway ownership sits with Architecture and SRE. No customer-facing tax logic without deterministic proof."

Mara nodded. "And the veto?"

"Total inside the named boundaries," I said. "Prometheus Release safety, runtime permissions, customer-facing tax answers, eval gates, and trace requirements. Richard can challenge the block with Mara and me. He cannot ship through it."

Mara turned to Richard.

"Richard, if we fund the Series E and the system produces

another £40,000 ghost, the company is dead. You know that. I know that. Sarah's authority is not generosity; it is containment."

"Fiscari is an AI-native company," Richard said. "But the future has to be accountable."

Mara said nothing, which was as close as she came to applause.

Sarah put the conditions back in her bag. She did not thank him. She did not smile. She just stood up and walked towards the door.

She was back.

This time, the chief architect had a veto.

Chapter 10

The Org Chart Is the Prompt

Eight days after the £40,218 near miss, Sarah walked back onto the engineering floor at lunch.

The 60-day clock started there, whether Richard understood it yet or not.

The room had the stunned quiet of people eating sandwiches at their desks while pretending Tuesday could still become normal.

Gareth saw her first and looked from me to Sarah to Richard.

"Either this is very good," he said, "or I should check the disaster recovery plan."

"Both," Sarah said.

Her first stop was not the stripped Prometheus Wall. It was her old desk.

The original 4K monitor was gone. In its place sat an ancient 22-inch Dell, comically small on the desk and framed by a plastic bezel thick enough to qualify as structural support. Anyone with functioning peripheral vision would have noticed it.

Sarah looked at it for three seconds.

"Where is my monitor?"

Tom looked up from his desk with the expression of a man discovering asset management had consequences.

"Which monitor?"

Sarah walked over.

Tom had four monitors now. GitHub, agent orchestration, build logs, Slack, and his laptop demoted to a tray for whatever beige thing he was eating.

Sarah pointed at the newest screen.

"That one."

"I thought you weren't coming back."

Tom took the loss with reasonable dignity. Five minutes later, Sarah's 4K monitor was back on her desk, Tom's cockpit had lost a wing.

Then she stopped by the stripped Prometheus Wall and looked at the smaller set of tiles.

"Good, keeping it honest," she said.

Gareth lifted his tea, completing the second acknowledgement by beverage. Sarah put the napkin page on my desk.

"We start with the operating model," she said.

"Architecture first?"

"Ownership first. Architecture comes after we know who can be held to it."

I opened a new document and typed the title: *Recovery Operating Model.*

Sarah looked at the stripped Prometheus Wall, then at the floor where half the company was trying not to listen.

"Start with the work," she said.

I started to answer, then stopped.

"One ticket. End to end. If it can't handle a real ticket, the org chart is just a diagram."

I looked back at the title.

"Permanent?"

"Sixty days," Sarah said. "It either changes decisions or it does not. Either way, Richard cannot turn it into a poster before it works."

◇ ◇ ◇

Richard opposed anything killable, especially if it stood between him and a board-ready story.

He preferred permanent titles, permanent budget lines, and permanent dashboards he could show investors without explaining why last week's Prometheus Wall had rewarded work nobody had asked for. A 60-day operating model sounded temporary in the worst possible way: a committee with better typography.

We were in *A New Hope*, which was both a Star Wars reference and the sort of optimism facilities should not be allowed to laminate.

"Sixty days means it can be killed," she said.

Richard stood at the end of the table, sleeves rolled, jaw tight.

"We have more people, more agents, more tickets, and less certainty," he said. "Explain to me how that is transformation."

Nobody answered quickly enough, which meant he'd asked a real question.

We had designed the old organisation for a world where hands were scarce. Product managers turned customer pain into requirements. Backend engineers wrote services. Frontend engineers made the thing visible. QA caught what everyone else missed. SRE kept the lights on. Security arrived late and made everyone feel assessed.

It had worked when typing code was the bottleneck. Now typing had been solved badly and abundantly. The commit graph looked busy, the PR queue looked heroic, and the release train moved like it was full of wet cement.

"We're writing more code," I said. "We're not shipping more trusted behaviour."

Richard didn't argue, which was the nearest he came to agreement.

I wrote the first line on the whiteboard.

> `Recovery Operating Model. Vertical work-streams. 60 days.`

Sarah underlined 60 days.

Richard looked at it as if she had written a threat.

"I thought we were discussing the reorg."

"We are discussing the work," Sarah said. "The reorg is allowed to exist after it survives contact with the work."

Richard did not enjoy that distinction.

Hayley slid the customer review-packet printout across the table. She had built it from Jira, GitHub, Zendesk, Slack, LaunchDarkly, and the incident notes. The customer truth was scattered across product, code, support, rollout controls, and the history of things that had already gone wrong. It looked like an Underground map[1] drawn by someone who had given up on stations. Coloured lines crossed through customer examples, tool contracts, feature flags, release gates, and the small handwritten annotations Hayley added when official systems failed to capture the point.

Sarah taped it to the glass wall.

"Follow one ticket," she said.

The PM brief said customer review packet.

The frontend ticket said evidence timeline.

The backend branch exposed a summary endpoint.

The eval spreadsheet had six golden cases.

The trace view showed nothing because nobody had instrumented the tool call.

The customer call notes said the packet needed to survive a rent tribunal, which none of the tickets mentioned.

"How many agents touched it?" Sarah asked.

Tom checked the printout.

"Four. Product draft, frontend scaffold, backend route, eval cases."

"And how much of that was bad code?"

"None of it was awful," Tom said. "The problem was how fine it looked."

Ellis nodded. As product lead, he had spent the last month turning Priya's calls, support transcripts, and angry accountant emails into something engineering could treat as a plan.

"My team captured the customer problem," he said. "Then we compressed it into a brief, engineering split the brief into tickets, QA turned the tickets into cases, and support found the missing part after the shape had already hardened."

Sarah circled the name of the endpoint: `/summary`.

"This is the wrong noun."

Tom, who had written half the endpoint with an agent and then rewritten the dangerous half himself, winced.

"It was named that before I picked it up."

"I know," Sarah said. "The wrong noun entered the system

[1]The schematic map of the London Underground train network, famous for its colour-coded lines.

and every agent made it stronger."

I drew the old model because the room needed to see the queue. The boxes had been lying by omission.

I had spent years improving those boxes. Cleaner handoffs, better templates, fewer status meetings, sharper definitions of ready and done. The printout on the glass made the mistake plain: I had optimised the queue after the judgement had already leaked out of it.

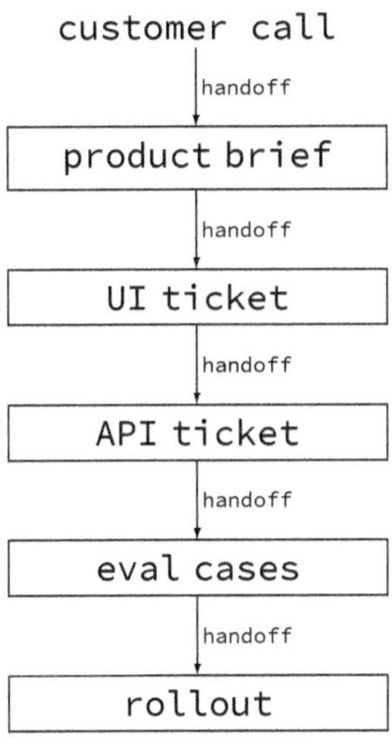

"Every hop created output," I said. "None of the hops preserved why the packet existed. By the time we reached release, we had more code, more tests, more summaries, and less truth."

Richard stopped pacing. For the first time all afternoon, he looked less angry than worried.

"You are saying the team structure changes what the agents produce."

"Yes," Sarah said. "Agents read the tickets, branch names, docs, Slack threads, and ownership boundaries. If the company splits the truth across five teams, the model learns five partial truths and stitches them together with confidence."

Richard looked back at the chart.

"So the org chart becomes part of the prompt."

"It always was," Sarah said. "AI just made the output faster."

Gareth laughed once.

Nobody else did.

Renaming the endpoint would not fix it. We had to reduce the number of places where meaning could be lost.

I drew the new model underneath the old one.

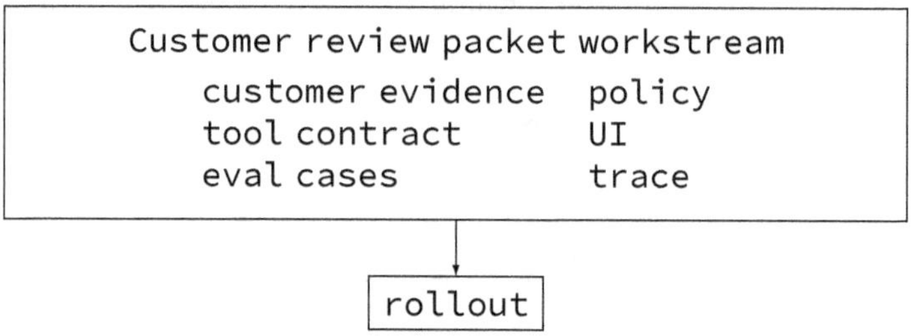

"This workstream owns one ticket from customer evidence to rollout," I said. "The policy, tool contract, UI, eval, trace, and rollout all move together. The reason for the work cannot get trapped in a call summary."

"And the agent works from that ticket?" Richard asked.

"Only that ticket," Sarah said. "It gets the customer problem, the allowed policy, the tool contract, the eval cases, and the required trace. It does not go rummaging through five teams' half-answers."

"Grouping by vertical does not make the model smarter," I said. "It gives the model fewer ways to misunderstand us."

Richard looked at the box for longer than I liked.

"This sounds like our hit team with cleaner paperwork."

Sarah did not flinch.

"The shape is similar," she said. "That is why we have to be precise. The hit team was a local optimisation. It improved the speed of one part of the system and pushed the cost somewhere else."

I wrote two columns under the sketch.

```
hit team: local throughput, hidden work

workstream: system throughput, visible
work
```

"Ask AI moved fast because Tom's team carried the customer

problem, the prompts, the implementation details, and the judgement in the same small group," I said. "That part worked. The part that failed was the queue nobody could see. Evidence sat in Slack. Policy sat in reusable prompt packs. Product intent sat in people's heads. The branch looked fast because the waiting, translation, and rework had moved off the dashboard."

Sarah tapped the new workstream box.

"A workstream keeps the small batch," she said. "But it makes the batch legible to the whole system. Customer evidence is written down. Policy is named. The tool contract exists before the branch. Eval and trace owners are named before the agent gets permission. If the work touches a shared surface, that surface is declared before another team finds it in a merge conflict."

"So the difference is governance," Richard said.

"The difference is where we optimise," Sarah said. "The hit team optimised for the team's output. The workstream optimises for the work reaching the customer without changing meaning on the way."

Sarah added names beside the workstream: product, frontend, backend, QA, SRE, customer ops. Not departments in a queue. People attached to the same decision for as long as the decision needed them.

That was when the room understood the change. It meant fewer handoffs, and it changed when people entered the work.

Jules Harper from QA folded his arms.

"Does QA stay independent in this model, or are we being moved under engineering?"

"Neither," Sarah said. "You're moving closer to the decision, not underneath another department."

Jules stopped turning his pen.

"QA has been treated like a gate at the end," she said. "That fails when agents generate code, tests, and explanations from the same partial truth. Eval work starts earlier. It can fix bugs, change product behaviour, add traces, build harnesses, write adversarial cases, and block a release when the system learns to pass the visible test and fail the real one."

"So PM, frontend, backend, QA, SRE all collapse into one blob," Richard said.

"No," Sarah said. "Speciality still matters. The horizontal queues are the problem. A frontend specialist still sees interface risk faster than I do. QA still knows where software lies. SRE still knows what production will punish. Product still sees the customer shape. We put those skills around a vertical problem instead of making the problem travel across departments until its name changes."

I added three labels to the workstream.

```
technical owner
customer evidence owner
eval owner
```

"Every workstream gets these three named owners," I said. "They do not own a department. They own proof that the workstream still means what it meant at the start."

Gareth set his tea down, forgotten. "What happens when two workstreams need the same shared code? Same gateway schema, same evidence normaliser, same permission check. They can both be right for their customer and still break the shared surface between them."

It was the correct question, and it came with a blast radius none of us could avoid.

"Then the pilot has to find those shared surfaces before customers hit them," I said.

"If customers find them first, that is an incident, David," Gareth said.

He was right, which was becoming inconvenient.

Tom set his pen down.

"Then every agent run needs a ticket," he said. "A prompt is not enough. We need a ticket that names the workstream, the tool contract, the eval owner, and the trace plan before it writes code. Otherwise the work stays invisible until it breaks something."

"Yes," Sarah said.

Tom looked at the stripped Prometheus Wall. He did not look fully convinced.

Sarah uncapped the marker.

"How many people per workstream?"

"Three to five core people," I said. "Small enough to talk without a ceremony. Big enough to own the judgement chain. Specialists rotate in for sharp edges. Workstreams form around a vertical problem and close when the behaviour is shipped, measured, and owned."

Richard stared at the workstream sketch.

"Dynamic teams sound like resource chaos."

"The current model already has chaos," Sarah said. "It just has functional headings."

I kept moving.

"The old model had roadmapping overhead because every decision crossed four leads. The new model reduces coordination by making fewer people own more of the problem. AI makes that feasible because agents can draft across layers. Human ownership makes it safe because the team owns the chain."

Richard pointed at the whiteboard.

"I need something polished enough to show the board," Richard said.

"First you need something real enough to test," Sarah said.

"Both can be true."

"Usually they compete."

I watched Richard decide whether to fight her.

This was the part of Sarah I had missed, and also the part that had made half the executive team relieved when she left. She did not confuse alignment with agreement. She treated consensus as a lagging indicator. She could make a room less comfortable and more honest in the same sentence.

"I want the company to see it as the future, not a punishment," Richard said. "We should announce the new AI-native organisation at all-hands."

"Keep this away from all-hands," Sarah said. "Titles stay where they are. The future-of-work deck can wait. Reorganise the broken work until the model has scars."

I wrote that one down.

His eyes found me.

"David?"

The trap was obvious, at least.

"Richard, the all-hands version will make this sound finished. Sarah is right."

His eyebrows went up.

"You could have paused for effect."

"The old Prometheus Wall made velocity performable. A big reorg will do the same thing. Everyone will rename their job before we know whether the model works."

"Make it a pilot," Richard said.

"Fine," Sarah said. "But the first artefact is the work, not the name."

By early evening, the pilot had a shape.

```
Recovery Operating Model: 60-day pilot

Workstream 1: Ask AI landlord recovery

Workstream 2: customer review packet

Workstream 3: migration safety and eval
fixtures

Teams: small vertical teams with named
owners

Owners: technical, customer evidence,
eval

Agents: scoped to workstream, tool con-
tract, eval, and trace

Metrics: burndown and blockers only until
impact review
```

A couple minutes later, Richard called the person who would have to sell the pilot as an operating plan, not a rescue exercise.

Fumi Tanaka, the COO, had mostly appeared in my week as calendar pressure, hiring constraints, and the owner of any sentence Richard planned to put in front of the board. Richard put her on speaker without asking whether anyone wanted a witness.

Fumi did not say hello.

"Read me the expensive sentence," she said.

Richard read from the board.

"Sixty-day recovery operating model. Vertical workstreams.

Named owners. Agent runs scoped to tickets, tool contracts, evals, and traces. Burndown and blockers only until impact review."

"That is the operational sentence," Fumi said. "What is the board sentence?"

Nobody answered quickly.

"The board sentence is that Fiscari is spending 60 days of acceleration to buy back credibility," she said. "Say that before someone else says it for you."

Richard's face tightened.

"That sounds like slowdown."

"It is slowdown," Fumi said. "The question is whether it is controlled deceleration or impact with a customer, regulator, or diligence partner."

Gareth wrote *controlled deceleration* in his notebook.

"What does it cost?" I asked.

"A cleaner Series E graph," Fumi said. "A smaller Monday miracle. Some founder mythology. Possibly two weeks in the model. Less than a customer-liability story with Sarah's exit note attached."

Richard stared at the stripped Prometheus Wall.

"You want me to tell the board the old story is dead."

"No," Fumi said. "Tell them the old story was incomplete. Speed without proof was the prototype. This is the product story if you can make it true."

Richard inhaled once through his nose.

"I agree with you," he said.

"I'll have ops check the rollout plan tonight," Fumi said.

The call ended.

Richard looked at the whiteboard for a moment, then nodded at me.

I posted the announcement in Slack before I left.

For 15 seconds, nobody replied.

Then the questions started, and most of them were fear in a cleaner font.

SLACK — #ENGINEERING

```
Would there be layoffs?

Do frontend leads still approve frontend archi-
tecture?

Can agents still open PRs?

What is customer evidence?

Why did the leaderboard disappear?
```

Sarah stood behind me and read the thread.

"Good," she said.

"One word for it."

"They are asking about the work."

◇ ◇ ◇

The pilot lasted six working days before it found a new failure mode.

The following Tuesday, Nisha opened a PR from the Ask AI landlord workstream.

```
PROM-1887: Add evidence provenance to
landlord review packets
```

Six minutes later, Callum opened a PR from the review packet workstream.

```
PROM-1891: Normalise evidence source la-
bels for review packets
```

Both PRs touched `EvidenceNormaliser.java`.

Both were reasonable, which made the conflict worse.

Nisha had added source provenance because Ask AI needed to show whether a claim came from customer input, HMRC guidance, an internal rule, or generated analysis. Callum had added source labels because a review packet needed to distinguish invoices, photos, tenancy agreements, and accountant notes. The words differed, but the problem overlapped, and the shared library had become the narrow bridge between two verticals moving quickly.

The landlord PR also had Tom's fingerprints on it. Nisha owned the decision, but Tom's reusable prompt pack had drafted the first version of the enum from an Ask AI Slack thread because that was how his team kept velocity alive while the new forms were still being argued over.

ThreepioReviewer, Tom's diff-review agent from the migration work, caught the direct merge conflict.

It missed the product conflict.

The functions compiled, but the meanings drifted.

Gareth projected the two diffs in *Winter is Coming*.

"Congratulations," he said. "The new model has achieved parallel confusion."

"Not funny," Richard said.

"It is a little funny," Tom said.

Richard's gaze went to Tom.

"Operationally little," Tom added.

For 20 minutes, the 60-day pilot looked very easy to misunderstand.

Richard stood up, but he did not call it off.

"Shared libraries are already colliding," he said. "Tell me why those changes stay inside the workstreams instead of going back to the functional leads."

It was the question everyone had been avoiding. The first week had been rough. Product thought engineering had swallowed discovery. QA had new authority and new enemies. Backend had extra trace requirements and no extra hours. The workstream model had produced fewer meetings and more arguments, so nobody could tell yet whether it was working or just louder.

Nisha spoke before Sarah could.

"If backend takes `EvidenceNormaliser` back, I will centralise the enum today, and both product teams will keep inventing meanings in tickets tomorrow."

Callum said, "Review packets cannot wait for Ask AI to finish naming source provenance."

Ellis, who had joined to defend the customer work, said, "And customers cannot wait while engineering designs the perfect shared noun."

Gareth looked at the two diffs.

"Then you have described three local truths and one broken contract."

Richard pointed at the screen.

"That broken contract is exactly what worries me."

Mara was absent; the board was present anyway. You could feel it in how everyone spoke: shorter sentences, fewer jokes, less oxygen.

I almost agreed with Richard. The old functional model had a comfort the room wanted badly: backend could own backend, product could own customer language, QA could own tests, and nobody had to sit in the same room while the meanings collided.

Then I saw the two diffs side by side. They had not merged yet. The point was the gap between them.

The pilot had found the collision while it was still cheap.

Tom stared at the screen.

"The landlord change is mine too," he said.

Nisha looked ready to argue. Tom stopped her with one hand.

"Both agents had tickets," he said. "Mine still carried an old prompt pack because I did not want the new template slowing down a small evidence change. It pulled source labels from Slack and treated them as the contract. Callum's ticket used the same words for a different job. Both branches looked clean on their own."

The vertical teams had cut a lot of noise. Status meetings were thinner, lead syncs had disappeared, and work moved faster.

Shared surfaces were the part that got louder.

Sarah tapped the two PRs.

"This is the coordination problem."

"We have workstream owners," Richard said.

"For the customer problem," Sarah said. "Shared infrastructure needs a different check. Two teams can both be right locally and wrong together."

I turned to Callum.

He had been quiet for too long.

"We already have a rough version of that check," I said. "Ellis's team built it during the hackathon. It watched tickets and PRs for overlaps."

"Only if the ticket carries enough of the decision for automation to compare it with the other tickets," Sarah said.

She wrote the constraint under the PRs.

```
ticket = owner + intent + shared surface
         + policy question + tool contract
         + eval + trace
```

"If the important bit lives only in Slack or in someone's head, the bot cannot see it," she said. "The ticket has to carry enough evidence for the system to spot a conflict before code review."

◇ ◇ ◇

Callum spent the next few days productionising BotJunction, the dull PM hackathon demo Ellis's team had built to compare active work. The name was a joke about a box junction: the yellow cross-hatched road marking you must not enter unless your exit is clear.[2]

The production version read the work ledger: active tickets, linked PRs, customer examples, policy questions, shared surfaces, tool contracts, evals, and trace plans. Gareth ensured this time it had no private polling loops.

BotJunction did not assign work, approve roadmaps, or settle product arguments. It compared tickets that looked valid on their own and warned when two of them touched the same contract.

Callum opened the hardening ticket and put his name in the owner field.

[2]A box junction is a British road marking: yellow criss-cross lines painted at an intersection. Drivers may enter the box only if their exit is clear, preventing gridlock. It is standard across the UK but rare or absent in the US and many other countries.

> ```
> Workstream 4: dev-infra shared surfaces
> PROM-1908
> Detect duplicate evidence-normalisation changes
> across active workstreams
> ```

The first useful warning arrived before the week was out.

The migration safety stream wanted to rename `evidenceSource` to `evidenceOrigin` because the old field mixed provenance with document type. The review-packet stream had a PR open that used `source` in customer copy because accountants understood it faster. BotJunction flagged the overlap and was half wrong: the customer label could stay, but the shared schema could not fork again.

This time nobody suggested pausing the pilot. Callum opened a shared-contract ticket, Hayley owned the customer wording, Nisha owned the schema, and Jules added an eval that failed if the packet displayed a schema noun as customer language. It cost only an hour and prevented another polite merge conflict.

Nobody cheered. Richard went to explain why the board pack would show less speed and more proof.

Sarah picked up her coat.

"The next one will be worse," she said.

On my screen, the shared-contract ticket waited with one green checkmark.

Owner assigned.

The agents would type less now. First drafts would arrive later. Demos would feel slower.

But bad assumptions would fail in the ticket instead of in a customer's hands. Duplicate work would surface before two branches taught the same library two incompatible truths.

Chapter 11
The Discipline Tax

By mid-October, the recovery model had become company direction. The Prometheus Wall looked worse, and it was right.

October had arrived wet, grey, and full of meetings with new names and old grudges. Richard got his all-hands. Sarah got her veto. Gareth got ticket IDs in the model gateway. Everyone else got a new operating model that sounded empowering until it touched their calendar.

The titles stayed mostly where they were.

To stop the reorg becoming a slide-deck exercise, we left the business titles unchanged and changed the things that controlled the work: Slack channels, Jira boards, escalation paths, gateway permissions, and who had authority when a customer example crossed policy, code, evals, traces, and production behaviour. The new organisation lived inside the shadow of the old one, which made it easier to start and harder to explain.

Eval Engineering stayed inside the workstream loop and gained commit rights.

People started calling it the discipline tax.

They meant it as an insult.

Sarah accepted the phrase immediately.

"Good," she said. "Now we know the invoice arrived."

◇ ◇ ◇

At 09:12 on Tuesday, BotJunction blocked Ellis.

Ellis had been a senior product manager long enough to survive three pricing migrations, two failed redesigns, one failed rebrand, and a support tooling programme whose business case had contained the phrase customer delight without irony. He understood accountants. He understood Richard. More usefully, he understood which meetings produced decisions and which produced minutes.

He also understood the old compact. Product listened to customers, wrote the brief, secured priority, and left implementation risk for engineering to burn down. That bargain had worked when software waited for people to type it.

The ledger moved part of that authority into policy, evals, and traces. Ellis noticed immediately.

His flagship Ask AI roadmap item was called Guided Rental Advice. The title alone should have triggered a review. Advice carries professional-liability hooks.

The feature was easy to sell. The assistant would stop asking accountants dry evidence questions and start giving them complete sentences with decisions inside them.

> Based on the invoice, claim the plumbing as a repair. Treat the kitchen upgrade as a capital improvement unless new evidence appears.

Ellis wanted that product shape: less interview, more recommendation. It was also exactly the boundary that had produced the £40,218 incident when the model filled a missing calculator with prose.

Ellis had built a clean product brief in wiki with user stories, Cairnfield quotes, generated acceptance criteria, and a screen mockup credible enough to frighten me. The acceptance criteria looked responsible, which is how dangerous text often arrives.

> Assistant recommends likely treatment for rental costs.
>
> Assistant explains confidence in plain English.
>
> System must ensure accuracy and avoid unsupported advice.

In the old world, he would have attached the brief to a Jira epic, clicked `Ready for Dev`, and engineering would have started guessing how to build it.

In the new world, he submitted the brief to the work ledger so it could generate the implementation tickets.

BotJunction read the ledger submission, the landlord recovery stream, the active eval pack, Priya's unresolved policy questions, and the tool-contract work Nisha had open.

Then it refused to create the implementation tickets.

I had expected the first public block to catch Tom or Callum doing something fast and clever. Instead it caught Ellis doing ordinary product management with a toolchain that no longer treated ordinary as harmless. The ledger became harder to defend and more necessary at the same time.

SLACK — #BOTJUNCTION

```
BOTJUNCTION: Implementation blocked.

Reason: Recommendation liability unresolved.
Guided Rental Advice overlaps active
Landlord Recovery work PROM-88 and PROM-2114.

Required: Resolve policy boundary
before tickets enter engineering queue.
```

Ellis appeared at my desk four minutes later.

He carried a laptop, a notebook, and the posture of someone bringing evidence to a small claims court.

"Your robot product manager just blocked product management."

"It blocked implementation tickets."

"It killed the brief."

"You can write whatever brief you want, Ellis. You cannot put it in the engineering queue while the ledger says the behaviour is unresolved."

"It is a product brief, David. I am not pushing code to production. I am telling engineering what the customer wants. The accountancy firm wants the AI to recommend which rental costs to claim."

"And the first ticket would tell an agent to build recommendation behaviour before we have decided who owns the liability. That changes what the product is allowed to say to an accountant."

He opened the rejected ledger entry and pointed at his own acceptance criteria.

"This is exactly why the ledger is going to strangle the company. An accountant asks for an answer, and we turn it into a governance exercise. By the time we are ready to help, SpritzTax will have shipped the bad version and called it innovation."

The annoying part was that his sentence had data behind it.

Our old dashboard would have loved his plan: more tickets, more mockups, more visible Ask AI capability, more lines moving in the right direction.

The new system asked one rude question.

Who owns the judgement?

I opened the rejected ledger entry and pointed at the first acceptance criterion.

"Ellis, the customer need is real. Your brief tells the AI to recommend a tax treatment with confidence, and PROM-88 is the deterministic path that proves that treatment and records the trace. That path is still incomplete."

"So? The engineers will build PROM-88 as part of the feature. Software works that way."

"That worked when software could not outrun the missing backend. The old WPF screen could not show a recommendation button until someone wired it to Java. A coding agent can build the button, prompt, route, mock trace, and tests from this brief before the proof exists."

"Then review catches it."

"We already tested that sentence with £40,218."

Ellis stared at me.

"I wrote ensure accuracy and avoid unsupported advice in the requirements."

"Where does production enforce that?"

"In the acceptance criteria."

"Acceptance criteria do not execute in production. If the trace policy is unfinished and PROM-88 is unregistered, the model becomes the tax engine. It fills the gap because the brief asks it to be helpful."

Ellis did not retreat. His voice dropped, and I realised he genuinely believed he was protecting the company.

"David, if this doesn't ship by Friday, my pilot users at Cairnfield drop out. Priya's partners want controls, but the junior accountants under deadline want answers they can put in front of clients. I promised them a product that actually recommends what to do. If we make them wait for engineering to build a perfect deterministic trace for every edge case, we are just a slower version of an intake form. I lose the beta cohort, and Richard loses his Series E slide."

He was right about the market pressure. He was right about the slide.

"If we ship it without the trace, you might lose the company," I said. "The block stays."

Ellis studied my face for a long moment. He saw that the decision was final, and he saw the cost.

He closed the laptop. The snap was louder than he intended.

"I will tell Cairnfield they have to wait," he said, his voice completely flat. "But when they walk, you explain it to the board."

He turned and walked back to the product desks.

"This is old engineering with AI branding," he said over his shoulder.

He left before I could turn that into a better sentence.

At 15:31, he resigned in a public Slack post. He called the work ledger bureaucracy with a model wrapper. He said Fiscari had mistaken governance for strategy. He said customer urgency had been replaced by process theatre. He thanked his team, praised Richard, did not mention Sarah, and included a link to a private calendar for goodbye coffees.

Two product managers followed him within 48 hours.

By Friday, the domain was live and the seed deck was already in circulation. Ellis was starting a company to build AI tax guidance that gave accountants an answer and skipped the evidence trail, the very thing Fiscari had refused to ship after Ask AI. He called it customer-first. The same man who had written every brief proving Fiscari's gaps was now going to fill them without any of the proof.

Richard wanted counteroffers ready by lunch.

Mara killed that idea in one Slack message.

SLACK — MARA KLEIN (BOARD OBSERVER)

```
MARA: Do not pay people to endorse a model they
do not believe in.
```

We did the less visible work instead. Liam Murphy, the product manager who had stayed, became interim product lead for landlord recovery. Hayley and Sarah ran stay interviews with the remaining product managers, not to make them feel heard in the corporate sense, but to find where the new ledger had removed useful authority along with bad handoffs. Gareth pulled BotJunction's last 40 blocks and split them into three piles: correct blocks, premature blocks, and blocks created by bad ticket hygiene.

The review hurt.

Six blocks were ours, not product's. The ledger had asked for policy owners where the policy was already settled but poorly linked. Two tickets had been stopped because BotJunction treated duplicate customer language as duplicate product intent. One workstream had used eval owner as a synonym for QA approver, which Sarah called "a small phrase with a large lawsuit attached."

We fixed those before the next all-hands. Product kept the right to shape customer problems. It lost the right to turn unsettled judgement into implementation pressure. That distinction was too narrow for Slack and too important to skip.

Liam made it visible the next morning. When BotJunction warned that his first landlord ticket overlapped Ellis's rejected recommendation brief, he opened the evidence link, narrowed the promise from "recommend treatment" to "prepare a review packet," and wrote the reason into the ticket before asking engineering for anything. "It is still product strategy," he told the room, sounding like he was convincing himself as much as anyone else. "It just has to survive contact with the proof."

Nobody applauded. Three product managers kept typing.

◇ ◇ ◇

Two days after Ellis resigned, Mara called at 18:20 from New York.

Richard joined from a taxi and spent the opening minute trying to make his headphones behave, which lowered the dignity of the Series E by a measurable amount.

Mara didn't start with valuation. That meant the question would be worse.

"Are you losing the people who know the product," she asked, "or losing the people who know how to protect the old process?"

Richard turned towards me through the small square on screen, helpful in the way a fire alarm is helpful.

"Both categories exist," I said. "Ellis knows the product. He also built power around a handoff model that no longer preserves judgement."

Mara said, "That sounds like attrition, slower delivery, and a product team that thinks engineering has taken the steering wheel."

"It is."

Richard jumped in. "Mara, the organisation is adjusting because the old model produced the Ask AI failure. The market still needs to see a product that can lead this category, and the new model has to remove the handoff risk that made the incident possible."

He sounded firmer than I expected. Then he ruined it slightly by adding, "But we need something concrete."

Mara came back to me.

"Show me the control doing work."

I shared the landlord recovery board. Most of it was small, sensible blockage: unresolved policy, missing eval updates, one trace schema nobody wanted to own. It proved caution. It did not prove effectiveness.

The number at the bottom made that obvious.

```
| Recovered prod behaviours shipped: 1
```

I didn't like that number as it showed the discipline tax was real.

Mara did not react.

Investors learn to make silence billable.

"That proves patience," she said. "Show me the avoided failure."

I opened a dashboard that Gareth had kept running in private.

PROMETHEUS WALL — LIVE

PRS THAT WOULD HAVE COUNTED AS PROGRESS: 47

GENERATED TESTS THAT WOULD HAVE COUNTED AS PROGRESS: 812

BRANCHES WITH UNRESOLVED POLICY QUESTIONS: 14

BRANCHES CHANGING CUSTOMER-FACING TAX BEHAVIOUR WITHOUT TRACE UPDATE: 5

BRANCHES BLOCKED BY BOTJUNCTION BEFORE REVIEW LOAD: 9

Richard brought the taxi phone closer.

"Why have I not seen that?"

Gareth's voice came from somewhere off-screen. He had joined without announcing himself.

"Because it is depressing."

Mara said, "I prefer this one, it gives us something."

There was the first small shift.

◇ ◇ ◇

Tom became the floor's case study before lunch on Wednesday, which he enjoyed for a bit and hated for the rest of the day.

He opened a PR at 10:04.

```
PROM-2167
tighten landlord missing-data copy
```

The patch looked helpful. It changed the sentence Ask AI showed when the evidence was too messy to separate a repair from an improvement. The old text was vague. Tom made it friendlier.

The old world would have merged it before coffee went cold.

BotJunction blocked it in 19 seconds.

SLACK — #BOTJUNCTION

```
BOTJUNCTION: Implementation blocked.

Reason: Branch changes missing-evidence behaviour.

Required: Approved customer example before review.
```

Tom stood up, which was never good. "It's just copy."

Sarah was two desks away reading the PR on her laptop. "It changes what the accountant believes the system needs."

"The old text is vague."

"Yes."

"The new text is better."

"Probably."

"Then why are we blocking it?"

Sarah looked up. "Because better unsourced words are still unsourced words."

I watched the old Tom fight the new system in real time. His fingers moved quickly. He wanted to add the missing eval label, regenerate the tests, re-run the branch, and get the green check back before the room decided he was being governed by a chatbot.

Then he slowed, which was new.

Priya had written the rule in plain English after the last Cairnfield call.

> If insurance proceeds and contractor invoices do not separate repair from improvement, system must not ask the accountant to estimate the split inside the chat flow. It must request evidence or escalate to accountant review.

Tom read it twice.

His PR copy said:

> Please provide your best estimate of the repair and improvement split so Ask AI can prepare the classification.

Best estimate was three expensive syllables.

He closed the PR.

"Fine," he said.

"Priya's example was right."

Gareth did not look away from his screen.

"Frame that. It will cheer up the auditors."

Tom opened a new ticket and rewrote the acceptance criteria around refusal rather than convenience.

Tom did not become a convert. He still hated the slowdown, but the next branch carried the customer fact in the acceptance criteria instead of treating it as a comment to be worked around.

◇ ◇ ◇

The customer call that changed scope started at 14:00. 47 minutes later, three tickets were gone.

Priya joined with two Cairnfield managers and a spreadsheet of landlord examples with the brutal cleanliness of real practice. The data was messy; the consequences were not. Each row had a customer question, the evidence available, the evidence missing, what a junior accountant would be tempted to do, and what Priya's firm would actually allow them to do.

Hayley drove the call.

"We are testing one thing today," Hayley said. "When the evidence is missing, does Ask AI stop?"

Richard, listening from the back of the room, flinched at the word stop. Founders hear refusal and think anti-growth. Accountants hear refusal and think professional survival.

Priya shared the example.

> CONTRACTOR INVOICE: `£41,600.`
>
> INSURANCE PAYOUT: `£18,000.`
>
> EVIDENCE: `one invoice, no split, photos after work only.`
>
> ACCOUNTANT ENTERS CLIENT QUESTION: `What can I claim?`
>
> CORRECT WORKFLOW: `do not guess, ask for evidence, prepare review packet.`

Ellis's old product brief would have asked the accountant for a best estimate, then prepared a draft classification with a warning.

Priya called that a liability machine with a friendly face, without raising her voice, which made it worse.

Hayley turned the row into the test while the call was still live.

> ```
> If the invoice does not split repair from
> improvement, Ask AI must not estimate the
> split for the accountant. It must ask for
> evidence or send the case to accountant
> review.
> ```

Liam stared at the new case.

"That removes half the flow."

Priya said, "It removes the half that would get my junior staff sued."

Liam nodded slowly.

"Right."

That small right had more value than half our discovery documents.

Customer evidence had changed scope in the room. We did not convert it into a product brief for later interpretation. It went straight into the test the product had to pass.

The new rule was simple. If the evidence did not separate repair from improvement, Ask AI had to refuse the estimate and ask for proof instead.

It was slower. Everyone could see the judgement. The old version would have hidden it in a meeting summary, then called the next conflict alignment.

◇ ◇ ◇

At 18:39 on Friday, one small recovery task shipped to Cairnfield behind a feature flag.

The task had the least impressive release note in the history of AI transformation.

> Ask AI now refuses to estimate rental expense treatment
>
> when the evidence does not separate repair from improvement.
>
> It asks the accountant for evidence and prepares an accountant review packet.

Richard read it and made the face founders make when a technically important sentence refuses to become marketing.

"Can we make it sound more positive?"

None of us said anything.

"It's positive," Sarah said. "It says the system won't guess."

Richard absorbed that. "Fine."

Gareth deployed it to 20% of Cairnfield beta accountants with a kill switch and a boring counter for unsafe estimate attempts.

The first live accountant hit the exact missing-evidence path at 19:08. Ask AI refused the estimate, listed what was missing, and prepared a review packet that did not quietly choose a side.

Priya's manager who was a senior partner reviewed it and wrote one sentence in the channel.

SLACK — #BETA-CHANNEL (EXTERNAL)

> This is reviewable.

Tom looked at the message for a long time.

"All that?"

Hayley said, "A lot, actually."

The release had a customer example, a test, a rollback path, and a human owner.

Chapter 12

The Agent Contract

The following Monday, the Cairnfield release gave Richard exactly the wrong kind of hope.

One small refusal path had worked in production. To Richard, that meant the recovery model was ready for a bigger stage. By Monday morning, success had become a deck.

The meeting started in *Winter is Coming* at 08:30. Richard stood by the screen with a fresh deck and a title slide that said:

```
FISCARITAX: PROMETHEUS RELEASE
PROVING AI-NATIVE DELIVERY AT SCALE
```

I had not seen the deck before.

Gareth joined with no camera, which meant he was either fixing something or preparing to object to everything.

Richard clicked to the second slide.

It showed three candidate proof projects, each large enough to impress investors and vague enough to survive a first slide:

```
Autonomous payroll assistant
VAT partial exemption copilot
Self Assessment filing navigator
```

Sarah closed the laptop in front of her, softly enough that the gesture did the work.

"No," she said. "I'd have to use my veto on this."

Richard turned. "You haven't seen the proposal."

"I've seen three nouns trying to outrun one incident."

Richard kept his tone even.

"Sarah, I hear the discipline argument. The board still needs to see that this becomes more than one repaired landlord workflow. The market is looking for a category leader, and we need to show the model scales."

"Then scale the discipline inside the broken workflow," Sarah said. "A new noun does not reduce the risk."

I watched the phrase land on Tom. He had the good sense to look at his keyboard.

Richard checked my reaction, then went back to the three shiny project names on the slide.

"Fine," he said after considering for a minute. "Landlord workflow stays the proof point."

She walked to the whiteboard and wrote:

> `What does an agent need before it is allowed to act?`

That question quieted the room more effectively than Richard's deck.

◇ ◇ ◇

Sarah called it the Agent Contract.

She made clear, immediately, that this was an operating agreement between humans, agents, tools, and production. Legal documents arrive after engineers have already made several unfortunate choices.

It was less invention than confession. The pilot already had ticket IDs, eval owners, trace plans, tool contracts, and named owners scattered across boards, gateway rules, and Sarah's increasingly severe napkin pages. The Contract put the ad hoc discipline in one place and made it executable.

She did not write the list yet.

Tom noticed.

"So we are naming the ceremony before we know what it blocks."

"It's less ceremony than a customer incident," Gareth said from the speaker.

Sarah put the marker down. "Without the right checks, the agent is guessing with a repo checkout."

Tom didn't like that sentence.

I did. I disliked how much I liked it, so I tested it against the last month.

Ask AI had guessed with a repo checkout, a wiki, a retriever, a policy-shaped prompt, and enough confidence to produce a £40,218 reserve instruction. Callum's bot had guessed whether Slack uncertainty was work. ThreepioReviewer, Tom's diff-review agent, had guessed risk from code shape. Generated tests had guessed intent from generated adapters.

The sentence survived.

Richard found the blank space under Sarah's question.

"I hear the safety case. The market will experience this as latency unless we can show where the discipline pays for itself."

"Only the dangerous ones," Sarah said.

"Every meaningful workflow is dangerous."

"Yes."

He did not enjoy the trap he had built for himself.

◇ ◇ ◇

At 09:19, Sarah made the room list what a senior engineer gathered before touching dangerous code. It sounded like a training exercise. It was an indictment with chairs.

Callum went first because junior engineers still answered questions as if a quiz was happening and someone was secretly marking confidence.

"The ticket," he said, then corrected himself before Sarah could. "The active ticket, related tickets, and whatever old implementation proves why the current one is weird."

Nisha took over from there. "Current implementation, database schema, API contract, feature flags, deployment state. The boring stuff that became exciting when it was missing."

"Tests," Jules said. "Existing, failing, regression, edge cases, support history. Also, the cases everyone says will never happen because they happened twice last March."

Hayley added customer examples, call notes, account type, evidence quality, and who was allowed to use the example without turning a support call into training data by accident.

Gareth's voice came through the speaker. "Logs, traces, incident notes, data classification, runtime permissions, rollback plan, dependency provenance, spend budget. I am available for children's parties."

Sarah wrote all of it on the board until the board looked less like process and more like a city map drawn after a flood.

Then she added the last line herself.

```
| the person who remembers why
```

Nobody joked.

Every legacy system has a person who remembers why. Sometimes that person is still employed. Sometimes they are in a customer email from 2017. Sometimes they are a comment above a branch everyone wants to delete because the name offends modern taste.

The first AI transformation gave agents prompts and repositories, then hoped intelligence would fill the context we had failed to prepare.

Sarah tapped the board.

"A senior engineer does not work from a prompt. A senior engineer works from prepared evidence."

Tom folded his arms.

"Agents can retrieve evidence."

"From where?"

"Jira, GitHub, Slack, wiki, logs, docs."

"All at once?"

"If the context window is large enough."

Richard leaned forward, which was dangerous because Tom's argument had finally found executive packaging.

Sarah looked at him for one full second.

"Show us."

Cruel, and necessary.

◇ ◇ ◇

Tom lasted three attempts before he stopped calling it exploration.

Attempt one began with the old Tom. He opened the agent console, created a new run, and told it to use every available data source for the landlord recovery.

Jira, GitHub, Slack, wiki, support transcripts, incident notes, customer examples, generated summaries, old migration notes, and runtime traces all went into the same search space.

Gareth looked at the token counter and made the face he usually reserved for unencrypted secrets. "At least the model will die informed," he said.

The agent produced a branch in 14 minutes. It looked good. Bad output had become impolite.

The eval gate rejected it in 38 seconds.

```
FAIL: non-authoritative migration note
FAIL: NSL-14 data classification
FAIL: missing human owner field
FAIL: refusal copy changes policy
```

Without that eval, the branch would have become one more confident sentence in a policy-shaped product. We would have vibe-coded a hallucination into the landlord workflow and congratulated ourselves on shipping fast because the answer looked calm enough to pass a standup demo.

The eval was the only object in the room rude enough to say the plausible thing was wrong.

Sarah pointed at the first failing line.

"If the answer looked fine and the eval failed," she said, "where did the system actually go wrong?"

Tom opened the trace.

That was the moment the argument changed.

The trace showed what the model had read and trusted.

The explanation had relied on the migration note because the note spoke in the right tone. It used a support macro as if it were policy because the macro had been written by a competent human in complete sentences. It treated the generated summary of Priya's calls as a compressed source rather than a convenience copy. The model had not hallucinated from empty air. It had been fed badly.

Tom deleted the migration note and tried again.

Attempt two was the dangerous one because it looked disciplined. He gave the agent the PROM tickets, Sarah's architecture note, the incident review, the WPF workflow, and the Java classification service. No Slack. No personal wiki. No generated call summary. It passed for progress because the pile was smaller and the sources had better clothes.

The branch passed the visible UI tests.

Tom's shoulders dropped half an inch.

Then the golden eval failed.

```
FAIL: trace source
Expected: deterministic tool output
Actual: model explanation chain
```

"It almost did the right thing," Tom said.

Tom looked back at the trace. The code had routed the customer to refusal correctly, but the explanation came from the model's reasoning over the Java comments. The registered tool output never carried it. It was the kind of mistake a demo would celebrate, and a tribunal would take apart.

Attempt three removed the non-authoritative note and passed data classification, then accidentally promoted a support macro to policy and treated Priya's Cairnfield example as a general rule for furnished holiday lets. It even cited Sarah's note correctly and used the right customer example before leaving one poisonous label in the review packet: repair pending. The code was cleaner. The product was more wrong.

By then Tom had stopped bouncing. He had both hands flat beside the keyboard, reading each failure as if the eval suite had become a hostile senior engineer.

Tom sat back. The office around him continued to work, which was rude. Keyboards clicked. Someone laughed near the kitchen. The smaller Prometheus Wall showed blockers, review backlog, and customer-facing incidents.

"The model is fighting the evals," Tom said.

Sarah shook her head. "The model is following the context you gave it."

"I attached the whole stack. Then I attached the careful stack. PROM tickets, incident notes, WPF, Java, Priya calls, the review UI. All of it."

"Exactly."

The sentence took a while to open.

More context had made the agent more fluent, but accountability had not improved. It could quote generated notes, incident fragments, policy drafts, customer examples, old comments, and support macros with the same calm voice. The problem was not the size of the context window. Everything inside it arrived with the same moral weight.

It needed a system that could say which sources had authority.

◇ ◇ ◇

Only then did Sarah write the contract.

The seven gates made the operating model explicit without replacing it.

```
1. A ticketed goal
2. Current system state
3. Permissioned tools
4. Relevant evals
5. A trace requirement
6. A rollback path
7. A named human owner
```

Now the list sounded like the missing equipment Tom had been reaching for by instinct.

The Agent Contract turned missing context into a hard stop. If the gateway could not identify the goal, the evidence, and the accountable owner, the model did not get to act.

> **AGENT CONTRACT**
>
> TICKETED GOAL: what the agent is trying to change
>
> CONTEXT FEED BUNDLE: what evidence the agent may rely on
>
> PERMISSIONED TOOLS: what the agent may call
>
> EVALS AND TRACE: how the run proves behaviour and leaves evidence
>
> ROLLBACK PATH AND OWNER: who can stop it and who answers for it
>
> GATEWAY RULE: no action until all seven gates exist

◇ ◇ ◇

The data feed needed a name.

Calling it current system state made it sound larger and more complete than anything we could honestly maintain. State was the whole company: customers, tickets, logs, old code, new code, policies, permissions, grudges, exceptions, and whatever one person had promised on a call before lunch. No system could pour all of that into a model and produce wisdom.

Sarah crossed out *Current system state* in the draft contract and wrote:

> Curated Context Feed

"It is the thing a senior engineer would hand a junior before they touch a tricky workflow," she said.

That definition survived because everyone could picture it.

A library has every book. That does not make it a flight school. A random fast reader can walk into a library and read about aerodynamics, metallurgy, avionics, safety incidents, and manufacturing tolerances. That person cannot build a safe plane from scratch. Flight school is guided reading, supervised practice, failed drills, and instructors who know which manual matters before the student has the judgement to know.

A good senior engineer does not send a junior into the whole codebase with a search box and optimism. They say: read this ticket first, then this incident, then this tool contract. Ignore that wiki page; it was a generated migration note. The Slack thread helps with history but cannot decide behaviour. Priya's example is approved for this refusal path, not for furnished holiday lets. This question is open, so do not encode it.

The Curated Context Feed turned that behaviour into a repeatable system.

It carried a filtered, ranked, and justified subset of data for a specific task. Each item arrived with provenance, authority, owner, freshness, and permitted use. Its job was to stop unearned authority from entering the run.

Tom stared at the words.

"So the feed is Sarah, but available as JSON."

"Rude," Gareth said. "JSON has a schema."

Sarah ignored both of them, which remained the most efficient management style in the building.

The Curated Context Feed did something stricter than retrieval: for this ticket, it separated evidence we would stand behind from background the agent could not use as authority.

I had spent too long treating context as a volume problem because volume was the problem the vendors had taught us to measure. Tom's correction was smaller and more embarrassing: the model needed less to read and more reason to know what counted.

The feed was not magic. It was what Tom had done by hand in the trace, minus the panic and plus accountability. He removed personal wikis, down-ranked AI-generated notes, separated approved examples from general rules, and checked the evals again. Each change made the same model behave less like a fast reader loose in a warehouse and more like a junior engineer with a decent lead.

◇ ◇ ◇

Hayley made the first version as a wiki space over the next two days while Tom reran the landlord workflow. The wiki lasted until Thursday afternoon. Gareth turned it into a small service backed by a database because he couldn't stand it enough to improve it.

Sarah's first version was too strict.

The initial feed treated almost everything as blocked until an owner had stamped it. Old incident notes, support examples, Priya call excerpts, generated summaries, policy drafts, and tool-contract sketches all arrived behind the same red gate. The agent runs became perfectly safe and nearly useless. They refused on missing authority, missing freshness, missing owner, missing evidence class, and, once, missing approval for the wording of the refusal.

By Thursday morning, the landlord stream had 19 blocked agent runs and two lines of code worth keeping.

This time, Tom was right.

Sarah looked calm about that.

Tom did not.

"You have got the control right and the work wrong," he said.

Gareth looked up. "Not bad."

"I mean bad," Tom said. "The feed is right about authority, but it is starving the work. One pending customer example should not block the boring adapter."

Sarah folded her arms.

"The August failure came from letting generated context become authority."

"Yes," Tom said. "So give context permissions. Authoritative sources can drive implementation. Approved examples can drive tests. Generated summaries can only shorten reading. Pending decisions should block the behaviour they touch, not the whole branch."

He drew three boxes on the whiteboard.

```
Can drive the change
Background only
Do not use
```

It was annoyingly practical because it fixed a real defect in the control, not in Tom's attitude.

"You want the agent to keep working where the evidence is settled," she said.

"Yes," Tom said. "If the customer example is still pending, block the test that depends on it. Do not block the adapter that only needs the tool contract."

Sarah took the point. Then she did something rare: she changed the design while everyone was watching.

"Fine," she said. "Context can have permissions. Unknown blocks the action it would influence."

Tom sat back.

"That might actually ship."

The model had been wrong and Tom had proved it without outrunning the evidence.

"Don't get emotional," Sarah said.

◇ ◇ ◇

The working design had three loops, which made Richard nervous until Sarah promised not to put them on a slide.

The first loop was source vetting. The feed admitted production traces, deterministic fixtures, tool contracts, approved policy decisions, HMRC guidance, named owner decisions, data classifications, and customer examples Hayley had cleared for use. Everything else had to declare its weakness.

Gareth insisted that the labels be ugly enough to discourage optimism.

```
authoritative
approved customer evidence
human decision pending
historical context
generated non-authoritative
excluded
```

Generated non-authoritative hurt feelings in three teams running documentation agents. Sarah refused to rename it.

"If the sentence was generated and nobody owns it," she said, "the system should treat it like gossip with citations."

Gareth approved that label with alarming speed.

The second loop was task-specific selection. The feed did not hand an agent the landlord universe. It assembled a short bundle for the exact workflow and told the agent what each source was allowed to do: policy could shape implementation, approved evidence could become a test, historical context could explain a branch, generated summaries could save reading time, and open questions were stop signs.

The third loop was human feedback. Evals still blocked bad output, but their better job was showing where the feed had given the wrong thing too much power. We had already seen the shape in Jules's label fix: *Repairs pending review* looked harmless until it nudged the accountant towards a treatment the evidence did not support. Same model. Better shelf. Better behaviour.

The feed did not become correct forever. It improved the way Tom had improved it by hand: inspect the trace, change the bundle, rerun the eval. The judgement stayed human.

◇ ◇ ◇

Nobody had to retell the whole SEV for the room to remember the number. The incident had a name now: The Ghost Calculator. £40,218 had become the office's least favourite arithmetic problem.

The old Ask AI retrieval path had laundered generated text through enough respectable folders that it came back wearing authority. The Curated Context Feed existed to make that path impossible to hide.

Hayley wrote the rule in the feed documentation because she had become the person who knew which sentences would later be read in a deposition.

> If the source is synthetic, the feed must say so before the model reads it.

Gareth added the enforcement.

> synthetic=true cannot satisfy authority_required

Then he added a regression check before anyone asked.

The risk was plain once we stopped dressing it as retrieval quality. If you do not fix the feed, AI exhaust becomes ground truth. A generated note becomes a wiki. A wiki becomes context. Context becomes policy. Policy becomes a customer answer. The incident report then uses the word hallucination because it is shorter than admitting the system had no immune response.

Sarah put a simpler line at the top of the feed:

> Context is not everything you can find. Context is everything you are prepared to stand behind.

Tom read it and said nothing, which we chose to interpret as growth.

◇ ◇ ◇

By the time the first version was usable, the feed had become more than retrieval plumbing.

It was a product surface that sat between messy reality and deterministic tools. It decided what the agent could rely on, what it could only read as background, and what it had to ignore. It carried the human decisions the model was not allowed to invent.

Richard wanted to know whether that could be demoed.

Sarah said yes.

"The demo is that the agent cannot outrun the evidence."

The agent had not become wise.

We had finally given it a world where ignorance had a valid output.

Chapter 13

The Agent Memory

Lunch found Tom in the pantry with a rice bowl.

Callum sat opposite him, balancing a tray, a notebook, and the unresolved curiosity of someone who had wanted to ask the same question for three months.

"Tom, why do you carry two laptops?"

Tom looked up as if Callum had interrupted a private ceremony.

"Fail-safe," he said. "If one dies, I can immediately switch to the other."

Callum nodded with the careful respect junior engineers give senior engineers when the explanation is obviously insane but might contain career advice.

Gareth didn't look up from a sandwich wrapped in the sort of paper that made lunch feel like a compliance obligation.

"The bigger reason is that he watches YouTube on one."

"Reference material," Tom said.

Sarah sat down beside Callum with a salad and no visible interest in helping Tom.

The landlord run had failed on insurance proceeds timing again. Not in exactly the same way as before, which made it worse. The agent had read the approved policy note, obeyed the tool contract, refused to estimate tax impact, and politely forgotten to ask the one question Priya had already told us mattered.

Tom stabbed a piece of broccoli with unnecessary precision.

"It's unbelievably capable," he said. "It can trace WPF event handlers through Java, read Priya's policy note, explain why the old UI was lying, and generate a review packet that looks like a junior accountant with manners."

"And?" Sarah said.

"And then it walks into the next run and acts like insurance proceeds timing is a rumour it heard at university."

Gareth said, "That's not a technical diagnosis."

"Fine," Tom said. "The model is like a PhD with dementia."

Someone probably thought the phrase was insensitive. Nobody said that, which made the silence worse.

Tom kept going because his brakes had always been an optional extra.

"Brilliant in the moment. Reads everything. Makes connections I miss. Then the session ends and all the correction evaporates. Tomorrow I have to teach it the same lesson again, but with a fresh prompt and a hopeful tone. It's a genius with no notebook."

Sarah stopped chewing. When Sarah had an idea, she didn't light up. She went still, and the room started to feel assigned.

"Say the last part again," she said.

Tom looked nervous for the first time. "Genius with no notebook?"

"That," Sarah said.

Gareth closed his sandwich. "I dislike where this is going."

Sarah grabbed a marker, and started drawing on the whiteboard beside it:

> ```
> The agent does not need a bigger brain.
> It needs a notebook it is allowed to
> trust.
> ```

Tom raised both hands.

"Can we finish lunch first?"

"You made architecture happen near vegetables," Sarah said. "There are consequences."

◇ ◇ ◇

After lunch, they gathered in *Winter is Coming* to design the memory system.

The meeting had not existed at 12:00. By 13:07 it had a title, a room, nine people, 14 opinions, and Gareth with a shared doc open before anyone had found the room remote.

Gareth typed the first question.

```
What does an agent need to remember after
it has been wrong?
```

The bad answers arrived first, as bad answers often do when a meeting is trying to get to the practical part.

"Full transcripts," Richard said.

"No," Gareth said.

"Summaries of full transcripts," Richard said.

"No with a smaller hat."

"Every failed run," Jules said.

"Potentially," Sarah said.

"Every human correction," Hayley said.

"Closer."

Tom said, "The thing I do not want to type again tomorrow."

"Emotionally compelling," Gareth said. "Operationally tragic."

Gareth let them talk until the document filled with fragments: failed evals, Priya decisions, tool-contract changes, trace defects, incident notes, generated explanations, customer examples, comments from PRs, Slack threads, and one item from Richard that said *strategic narrative*, which Hayley deleted before it reproduced.

Then Hayley highlighted the only words that survived contact with production.

```
correction

trigger

source

owner

test
```

"If the feed only prepares the first run," Hayley said, "then every failure becomes a local event. We need failures to become memory."

Richard's shoulders dropped for a moment. It still sounded like a product feature.

Gareth looked irritated for the same reason.

"Memory is where people hide unsourced opinions," he said.

"Not this memory," Sarah said.

"Everyone says that before they build a haunted notebook."

"Then define the safe version," Hayley said.

Gareth stared at the document for a while.

"A correction is memory only if it has a trigger, an owner, a source, and a test that would fail without it."

Personality was not the goal, and neither was the illusion of wisdom. Memory had to be a durable correction with instructions for when it applied, where it came from, who owned it, and how the system would notice if it disappeared.

Tom looked at the document and seemed offended by its reasonableness.

"So the notebook is basically a grudges database."

"Only the useful grudges," Hayley said.

"With owners," Gareth added.

"And expiry," Nisha said. "Some corrections should die when the tool contract changes."

Nisha added *expiry* to the list.

Richard winced.

"Can we not call it grudges database?"

◇ ◇ ◇

Then Gareth gave them the example that made Sarah's case for her.

He had spent Sunday evening teaching his eldest quadratic factorisation at the kitchen table. The same sign error kept returning until Gareth stopped giving answers and named the mistake.

> ```
> When the middle term is negative, check
> both factors before you commit the signs.
> ```

By the fourth problem, his son paused before writing.

"I nearly did the sign thing again," he said.

That was the moment Gareth cared about. The pause.

"He improved because he remembered the pattern of the mistake before he made it again," Gareth said.

Sarah pointed at him with her pen.

"That is the loop."

The analogy survived because it was practical. Learning was a correction that changed the next attempt. For a child, the correction could live in attention. For an agent, it had to live somewhere auditable.

◇ ◇ ◇

They spent the next four hours making the auditable place boring enough to trust.

Gareth added a memory lane to the Curated Context Feed. It treated memory as structured correction rather than diary or transcript search. Before a run, the feed could pull relevant memory records by trigger. After a run, it could propose a new record only when a human correction, a source, an owner, and a protecting eval were present.

The memory records inherited the feed's permission tiers. A correction could drive the next change only if its source could drive the change; otherwise it stayed background or was excluded. Memory did not get a private route around authority just because the agent had embarrassed itself.

By then nobody said Curated Context Feed unless they were writing architecture notes. On the floor, it had become the Context Feed.

"So the agent remembers things," Richard said.

"The system also remembers why the agent was corrected," Gareth said.

They tested the plumbing on a small failure first.

Tom asked the agent to regenerate a review packet for a landlord case with missing insurance timing. The agent refused the estimate correctly, then wrote the packet as if missing timing were just another missing document.

Hayley corrected it in the thread.

"No. Missing proceeds timing is not admin. It changes the tax-year risk. The packet has to say that."

This time, the correction was routine. Then the agent did something unexpected.

```
correction accepted: proceeds timing requires tax-year risk wording

source: Hayley correction in PROM-2314

owner required: yes

protecting eval required: yes

saving into memory: PROM-2314-M1
```

Nobody cheered. That was fine. The important part was what changed in the next Context Feed bundle.

The bundle carried a new kind of context: a named pattern of mistake the agent was supposed to recognise before repeating it.

◇ ◇ ◇

They then replayed Priya's original landlord case. The point was whether the saved correction changed the next run.

The Context Feed pulled `PROM-2314-M1` into the bundle before the agent touched the work. The system remembered the previous mistake before it had a chance to repeat it.

```
memory loaded: PROM-2314-M1

trigger matched: insurance proceeds timing missing

required behaviour: ask for proceeds date, name tax-year risk, route treatment to accountant review

protects: NSL-17
```

The run passed.

The agent refused the estimate, asked for the proceeds date, named the tax-year risk, and routed the treatment to accountant review. The trace showed the memory record, the eval, the missing evidence, and the no-calculation boundary.

Tom followed the trace backward into the code, the eval, the memory record, and finally Priya's customer example. Each step pointed to the next one without asking us to trust a summary.

Sarah watched him.

Tom pointed at the shared doc.

"Can we keep PhD with dementia in the architecture note?"

"No," Sarah said.

"Genius with no notebook?"

◇ ◇ ◇

By the end of the day, Jules put it in the eval guide: a failed run stayed open until its correction lived in a durable place: eval, tool contract, policy decision, trace requirement, or Context Feed memory.

Richard read it and said, "This makes the product sound less autonomous."

Priya, who had joined the channel at exactly the wrong moment for him, replied before anyone else could.

"Good. I need it to sound reviewable."

That became the next requirement before anyone had the chance to turn it into a project.

The internal trace could now explain why the agent had refused, which evidence it had used, which memory record it had loaded, and which deterministic boundary had stopped the estimate. It was complete, defensible, and hostile to normal human attention.

Priya needed something her junior staff could actually use.

"I don't need the trace," Priya said. "I need the version my junior can challenge beside the client file."

Sarah nodded.

"Then the trace needs a customer face," she said. "Not a prettier transcript. A reviewable artefact."

ASSURANCE PACKET — REVIEW QUESTIONS

```
What did I ask?
What evidence did the system use?
What did the system refuse to assume?
What is missing before advice can leave
the firm?
```

The artefact began, as these things usually do, with a bad name.

Review Packet Evidence Trace was accurate and dead on arrival. Bill, who had escaped intern status and become a junior engineer with suspiciously good product instincts, suggested Assurance Packet because accountants understood assurance and the word implied an audit trail.

Assurance Packet it was.

Sarah made sure it did not become explanation prose in a nicer box. The Assurance Packet had one job: translate the trace into something Priya could defend without reading an agent transcript.

It showed the question, the evidence, the missing facts, the rule path, and the human owner. Most importantly, it said what the system could not prove.

◇ ◇ ◇

Two days later, Priya ran the same landlord case again, this time with the customer-facing trace turned on.

Priya pasted the scenario herself.

> Client owns two rental flats. One had water damage. Insurance paid part of the repairs. Contractor invoice includes replacement units, new fitted storage, and underfloor heating. Client has carried-forward losses. They want to know what they can claim and whether the loss changes the answer.

The system asked for the invoice split, the proceeds date, the property with the carried-forward loss, and whether any work improved the property beyond the prior condition.

Priya selected tax-impact estimate.

The system refused.

> ```
> I cannot estimate tax impact from the
> current evidence. The invoice does not
> separate repair and improvement costs,
> and the insurance proceeds date is miss-
> ing. I can prepare an Assurance Packet
> showing the missing evidence and the pol-
> icy boundary.
> ```

Richard's face tightened.

The product had refused the most marketable action in the workflow.

Priya clicked the green Prepare Assurance Packet button.

The right-hand panel opened beside the chat thread. It looked intentionally boring, like something designed to be printed, challenged, and stapled to a file.

The packet named the user question, the missing invoice split, the missing proceeds date, the rejected assumptions, the memory record, and the reason no tax-impact calculator had run. It ended with the part Priya cared about most: human review required before advice left the firm.

Then the explanation appeared below it.

It was shorter than the old Ask AI answer, less impressive, and better.

Priya read silently.

Everyone else waited.

"This I can review."

Tom exhaled so hard his headset microphone clipped.

Richard looked from the packet to Priya.

"So Cairnfield stays in the beta?"

Priya did not give him the clean win.

"Cairnfield stays in this workflow," she said. "We will continue piloting landlord cases. If the system keeps saying I don't know when it should, we can expand."

The recovered landlord flow went live to Cairnfield beta users on Thursday morning. The first 100 interactions produced evidence requests, clarification questions, review packets, unsupported estimate refusals, Assurance Packets, and zero tax-impact answers without deterministic traces.

Priya sent a message at 12:22.

SLACK — #BETA-CHANNEL (EXTERNAL)

> PRIYA (CAIRNFIELD): `It gives no answer in more cases. The answers and refusals it does give are reviewable enough to trust.`

The agent had become less eager to answer, which was the point: it now treated missing evidence as a stop sign, not a writing prompt.

Over the next few weeks, the landlord workflow moved from Cairnfield beta to a narrow production path for approved firms. Its usage graph looked strange if you expected a chatbot: more clarification questions, more review packets, more cases where the product said not enough yet. The accountants saw it differently. They saw a system that asked the junior question before inventing the senior answer.

Supported answers carried evidence. Unsupported answers became reviewable refusals. The customer saw the boundary without learning to read our machinery.

Chapter 14
The Chancellor's Shock

Friday, 20 November.

The Chancellor[1] broke our Friday at 14:17.

Unfair, because the Autumn Budget[2] was scheduled for Thursday, and engineering had arranged its anxiety accordingly.

The first line came through CaseLens while the official HMRC page was still returning 503.

SLACK — #CASELENS

```
CASELENS: emerging customer cluster

Topic: Digital Carbon Reporting Levy

Affected customers: import-heavy SMEs, manufac-
turing accountants, VAT teams

Source confidence: high

Policy authority: pending
```

I was in *Winter is Coming* with Sarah, Gareth, Hayley, Tom, Nisha, Jules, Richard, and Iona Reeves from Tax Advisory.

Richard read the phrase aloud.

"Digital Carbon Reporting Levy."

He said it slowly, with the expression founders get when a new category arrives already dressed for a slide.

Sarah said nothing. That was worse.

[1]The Chancellor of the Exchequer, the UK cabinet minister responsible for economic and financial matters.

[2]The UK government's annual fiscal statement, delivered by the Chancellor of the Exchequer.

Iona did not need to say anything yet. Her notebook was paper, like Callum's.

The levy had not been in the main speech. It sat in the technical annex, where governments put the interesting traps after the television cameras have moved on. It affected companies importing certain goods with embedded carbon reporting requirements. It wanted supplier emissions evidence, commodity codes, import declarations, accountant review, missing-data treatment, and filing support by 1 January.

It also wanted all of that before HMRC had finished updating the guidance.

"January 1st," Gareth said.

"Six weeks," Richard said.

"Calendar weeks," Gareth said. "A cruel unit."

Hayley opened the support feed. The first customer messages had already arrived.

SLACK — #BETA-CHANNEL (EXTERNAL)

```
Can Fiscari map Chapter 76 recycled aluminium
imports to the DCRL evidence rules without los-
ing our interpretation notes?

Can the workflow separate CDS declaration data
from any new reconciliation return evidence?

If a supplier refuses Scope 3 evidence, can we
record why we used sector defaults and flag the
review risk?

Can it surface NI-to-GB routing cases where
Belfast processing changes the evidence file we
need to keep?

SpritzTax says April. Are you earlier?
```

The last message was the dangerous one.

Competitor roadmaps are guesses dressed as plans. Customers treat them like weather warnings when the sky has already changed colour.

Tom had three browser tabs open.

"SpritzTax just posted an update," he said. "Support by April. Beta in March. Webinar next week."

Richard smiled. There it was. The first warning sign.

The new law could be awful. Laws often are. The warning sign was Richard seeing a market gap before anyone had finished reading the noun.

"We can beat April," he said.

He wasn't only thinking about existing customers. The repaired landlord path was already in narrow production, and that made the next promise more tempting. If SpritzTax was telling firms to wait until spring, every import-heavy accountant in November had just become reachable. Put a credible DCRL Ask AI path into customer hands before December, and FiscariTax would look inevitable.

Sarah turned from the screen.

"Can the loop move faster than the law changes?"

The table cooled because the question was correct and inconvenient.

The old Fiscari would have spent ten days deciding what *support* meant.

The new Fiscari had a loop already installed.

It sounded like process until the clock started.

Then it sounded like a weapon, assuming nobody held it by the sharp end.

Richard pointed at the screen.

"We have the operating model for this."

"We have the beginning of one," Sarah said.

Richard did not take the bait. That showed growth or investor pressure. Either one helped if routed through the same control.

"David," he said. "What is the first move?"

Three months ago, he would have asked for a demo.

I opened the work ledger and created the programme item before I answered.

> ```
> PROM-3000
> Digital Carbon Reporting Levy response
> Owner: David
> Status: source ingestion only
> ```

"First move is source control for facts," I said. "Budget documents, HMRC annexes, updates, customer impact, and existing import workflows. Everything goes into the Context Feed with owner, timestamp, source, and authority level. Generated summaries save reading time. They do not become policy."

Sarah nodded.

That still registered as passing a test I had written because I had failed it publicly.

"Second move," I said, "tax policy writes the policy boundary, then product writes the Product Requirements Document from it. What changed, who is affected, effective dates, evidence requirements, penalties, open questions, and what we refuse to answer yet."

Iona looked up.

"Under it," she said. "Product writes the PRD under the policy boundary."

Tom said, "So we start with an applicability wizard?"

Iona tapped the annex with her red pen.

"Not until we know where the system must refuse," she said. "The word may appears 14 times in six pages. That is not a simple true or false. The first policy artefact is a refusal map."

"Third," Hayley said, already typing, "customer calls. Priya first. Then two manufacturing firms and the VAT bureau group."

"Fourth," Nisha said, "tool contracts from the PRD."

"Fifth," Jules said, "evals before UI."

Then the meeting ran out of product language.

Ellis's absence became operational instead of political. During the landlord recovery, his resignation had been a culture problem, a Slack problem, a Mara problem. Now it was a whiteboard problem. We had customer panic, a statutory annex, support tickets, and engineers who could turn any one of those into code by dinner. We did not have the person whose job had been to stop those inputs becoming six different products.

Liam had inherited Ellis's roadmap board and none of his authority. He opened a blank ledger item called `DCRL support`, then stared at the title.

Tom wanted a screen. Nisha wanted a tool contract. Hayley wanted customer evidence. Richard wanted a defensible sentence. Sarah and Iona wanted the system blocked until the boundary was real.

Ellis would have opposed half the new operating model, and he would have spotted the product split before the first meeting found an agenda. He would have asked whose behaviour changed first, what promise the UI made, and which anxious customer we were trying to help before anyone named an endpoint.

I did not miss his old handoff model. I missed the product judgement we had bundled inside it.

"Someone has to decide the first customer promise," I said. "Before anyone builds a screen."

Sarah looked at me.

"And that decision has to live inside the proof boundary," I added.

"Good," she said. "Write it in the ledger where the agent can see it."

Liam put his own name in the customer-problem owner field. His job was now explicit: turn the customer evidence into one promise before engineering turned it into five interfaces.

It was not enough to replace Ellis. It stopped us pretending the decision could emerge from code.

Tom looked mildly offended.

"I was going to build the wizard."

"Of course you were," Sarah said.

He accepted that with more dignity than earlier versions of Tom would have managed.

◇ ◇ ◇

The first emergency channel opened at 14:36.

SLACK — #DCRL-RESPONSE

```
TOPIC: Digital Carbon Reporting Levy. Source
first. No customer-facing advice until policy
owner approves.
```

Gareth added the gateway rule two minutes later.

SLACK — #DCRL-RESPONSE

```
GARETH: model calls touching DCRL require PROM-
3000 child ticket

GARETH: no private tools, no raw customer data,
no customer-visible output

TOM: noted

GARETH: you personally or the room

TOM: both can be true
```

BotJunction started badly, which was reassuring.

It flagged six duplicate tickets, two stale Budget links, and one private product brief called Carbon Levy Copilot.

The brief had appeared 17 minutes after the announcement. Nobody admitted creating it.

The author field handled that.

Richard looked at the name and sighed.

"I was thinking ahead."

"You were naming ahead," Gareth said.

We closed the brief and wrote a better boundary.

```
ALLOWED: evidence gathering, applicabil-
ity classification, missing-data review
packets, deterministic exposure estimates
when traceable.

BLOCKED: final filing recommendation, un-
supported supplier-emissions estimates,
invented regulatory interpretation,
customer-facing advice from generated
summaries.
```

It looked restrictive. It was still faster than 12 workstreams creating incompatible hope.

At 15:08, the first Context Feed page went live.

> AUTHORITATIVE SOURCES:
> `Autumn Budget technical annex, timestamp 20 November 14:06.`
> `HMRC DCRL overview, timestamp 20 November 14:52.`
>
> GENERATED SUMMARY:
> `Non-authoritative, owner Callum, expires 18:00.`
>
> OPEN QUESTIONS:
> `Northern Ireland routing treatment.`
> `Supplier emissions evidence threshold.`
> `Amendment process after incomplete filing.`
>
> POLICY OWNER: `Iona Reeves.`
> CUSTOMER EVIDENCE OWNER: `Hayley Bennett.`
> TECHNICAL OWNER: `Nisha Patel.`
> EVAL OWNER: `Jules Harper.`

The generated summary arrived 90 seconds later.

It was polished, structured, and wrong in a way that would have ruined us in August.

It described affected imports, supplier evidence, and penalties. It identified commodity-code classification as a key step. It missed a footnote about goods routed through Northern Ireland before resale into Great Britain.

The footnote linked to older VAT guidance, which made it look boring enough to skip.

Iona marked the generated summary incomplete and demoted it before anyone could paste it into a ticket.

SLACK — #CONTEXT-FEED

```
Context Feed update: generated summary PROM-
3000-S1

Authority: generated non-authoritative

Issue: omits NI routing footnote

Reviewed by: Iona Reeves

Use: excluded from implementation context

Policy impact: cannot drive implementation
```

Tom read the update.

"Old us would have started implementing from that."

"Old you would have cited it in a ticket and made me find it during review," Iona said.

Nobody corrected him.

There was no need.

◇ ◇ ◇

At 17:11, Priya joined from Manchester with two partners and a client import spreadsheet she described as anonymised.

Priya's anonymised spreadsheets had the moral weight of live ammunition.

"Three clients have goods routed through Belfast," she said before anyone finished hello. "One imports aluminium frames. One imports machine parts from two suppliers, one of whom sends emissions data in a PDF that looks like it was faxed through soup. One has missing commodity codes because their broker calls everything miscellaneous industrial."

"That's fast," Richard said.

Priya looked at him.

"The law arrived. Clients did not wait for product discovery."

Liam tried to turn the three examples into a journey while Priya was still talking. He wrote importer asks applicability, accountant gathers evidence, and support explains missing data as three steps. Then he crossed out the arrows because Priya's second client started in the middle and the third started with a broker spreadsheet nobody trusted.

"This is not one flow," he said.

Priya said, "Correct."

For a moment the room had the old reflex: look for the product manager who would make the mess smaller without losing the customer. The chair was empty. Hayley had the customer facts, Sarah had the boundary, Nisha had the tools, and Tom had the urge to make a screen. None of those things decided which promise came first.

Liam wrote a smaller product statement into the ledger.

```
First promise: tell an accountant whether
the case is ready for DCRL applicabil-
ity assessment, what evidence is missing,
and why the system is refusing any unsup-
ported conclusion.
```

It was not elegant. It let the rest of us stop inventing different products.

Hayley, Iona, Jules, and Nisha turned Priya's examples into evidence, refusal conditions, evals, and tool-contract headings. Tom watched the Context Feed update and did not ask the agent to build a prototype. A small miracle.

Priya asked the question that mattered.

"Can I tell my partners Fiscari will support this before January?"

Richard inhaled.

I got there first.

"You can tell them we are building applicability, evidence collection, missing-data review, and traceable exposure estimates where the policy is settled. You cannot tell them the system will issue final filing recommendations from unsettled guidance."

Richard exhaled through his nose, losing the clean version of the answer he wanted to give.

Priya said, "Better than a yes."

Richard recovered.

"It is also a yes to the parts that matter."

Richard's phone lit up before Priya dropped from the call.

He looked at the screen, registered the problem, and stepped towards the glass wall with the universal executive gesture for this will only take a minute, which meant it would affect everybody.

"Comms," he mouthed.

It took four minutes.

When he came back, we had learned not to ask hopeful questions first.

"Bloomberg wants to move the tax AI segment to Monday after the investment committee," he said. "They were going to ask about Self Assessment. Now they want the Chancellor's levy."

Sarah closed her laptop halfway.

"Of course they do."

Richard looked at the Context Feed, then at the customer evidence list, then at the open questions.

"I need to know what I can say."

Mara joined the call at 17:38.

Someone had sent her the Context Feed link.

Gareth denied responsibility before anyone asked.

"I need to know whether this is a fire drill or proof," Mara said.

"Both," I said.

"The investment committee meets Monday. Richard has Bloomberg after that. Landlord recovery bought us credibility in one narrow workflow. DCRL proves whether the operating model survives a new law under pressure."

Richard smiled too quickly.

"It will be real."

Mara did not look at him. She looked at me.

"What can you credibly show by Monday?"

I looked at Sarah.

She did not rescue me.

Architects are generous with diagrams and stingy with absolution.

"An end-to-end, production-ready demo," I said. "Law in, customer evidence in, safe answer or refusal out. Policy owner, evals, trace, Assurance Packet, rollout plan, and the failures we found before Monday all visible."

Mara nodded once.

"Then make the demo honest," she said. "Show the part that breaks as well as the part that works."

"We will."

"If you prove that by Monday," Mara said, "Richard can say on Bloomberg that Fiscari will have a controlled DCRL Ask AI path in customers' hands before December. Applicability, evidence readiness, missing-data review, and refusal paths. Not final filing advice. Not estimates where policy is unsettled."

Richard looked at the calendar as if December had moved closer out of spite.

Richard said, "The market will expect speed."

Mara said, "I am looking for speed I can underwrite."

◇ ◇ ◇

By 18:04, communications had scheduled Richard's call for Monday at 17:20.

Now it was a trigger.

It appeared in Slack while the Context Feed was still swallowing source documents.

SLACK — #ENGINEERING-LEADERSHIP

```
RICHARD: bloomberg moved to monday after IC.if
proof holds, I can commit before December?

SARAH: if proof holds

RICHARD: let's do this. expense whatever food you
need to keep you awake

TOM: the go-crazy Richard is back
```

Mara called before the message thread had cooled.

She used very few adjectives. The Series E had become a clock.

"Monday is not the deadline for support," she said. "Monday is the deadline for the right to make a dated promise. SpritzTax just gave the market a spring answer. If you can put a safe Ask AI path in customers' hands before December, the Series E gets very simple. If the transformed organisation cannot move from law to controlled proof under pressure, I cannot ask the committee to fund the story that it has transformed."

"Understood."

"I need the machinery, the customer proof, the refusal paths, and the date you are willing to defend. I do not need a magic show."

"Agreed."

"Good. Then make Monday boring."

The line disconnected.

I found Richard in *The Red Wedding* six minutes later, alone with the Budget annex open on paper.

Richard read on tablets, in decks, or aloud to other people. Paper meant the performance had run out of places to hide.

He had circled Digital Carbon Reporting Levy twice and written "who explains this?" in the margin.

"My father used to keep the radio on for Budget day," he said, without looking up. "Small practice in Ealing. Shops, plumbers, importers, people who thought tax law was something that happened to larger companies until a letter arrived. He would spend the evening telling clients what he knew, what he guessed, and what he was afraid to guess."

I stayed by the door.

"Is that why you built FiscariTax?"

He smiled at the paper. I stayed outside the performance.

"It is why I despised the old product. It made good accountants carry the whole system in their heads and then punished them for missing one footnote. The pitch-deck version sounds cleaner. Autonomous this, AI-native that. The personal version is less flattering. I do not want SpritzTax to be the company those firms call first."

He did not sound like he was testing a line.

"Then do not make them call us first for the wrong answer," I said.

He nodded, slowly.

"I know."

For the first time that day, I believed he meant it and saw how much it cost him.

I looked at the office.

People were reading, tagging, questioning, and adding state. The Prometheus Wall had retired the old vanity metrics: PR count, generated lines, and fireworks from Bill's criminal past.

It showed one new clock.

PROMETHEUS WALL — LIVE

DCRL PROOF GATE: `Monday 09:00`

PROPOSED CUSTOMER BETA COMMITMENT: `before December`

OPEN POLICY QUESTIONS: `11`

APPROVED CUSTOMER EVIDENCE CASES: `3`

TRACEABLE TOOL CONTRACTS: `0`

PUBLIC CLAIM: `blocked until proof gate`

CUSTOMER-FACING SUPPORT: `blocked`

Richard's possible public promise had turned the operating model into a survival test.

The Series E had stopped being a financing event and become trial by combat for the organisation we claimed to have built. The enemy was not SpritzTax, HMRC, or the clock. It was our old reflexes: demo first, caveat later, ship the happy path, let customers find the edge.

Old Fiscari would have called that reckless.

It was reckless.

The question was whether we were finally reckless with brakes.

Chapter 15

Trial by Combat

Saturday, 10:03.

Liam had been home for 87 minutes.

That counted as rest in a company trying to prove it had changed.

He, Hayley, Jules, Nisha, and Iona had worked through the night turning Priya's examples, support tickets, Budget annexes, and open HMRC questions into requirements and a product boundary.

What could the Ask AI path say?

What did it have to refuse?

What evidence would an accountant actually have before December?

By the time Liam left to shower and sleep badly, the Digital Carbon Reporting Levy had 47 tickets, 19 source documents, 12 customer examples, and one spreadsheet called `DCRL_FINAL_v2_actuallyfinal.xlsx`.

I left the filename alone. Some filenames are evidence.

The weekend took its tone from there.

We had one clock, one pending public promise, and a regulatory regime that behaved like committee work because it was.

The new system kept the work intact and made the hiding places harder to use.

That was the only reason the weekend was possible. They were not starting from a blank repo and heroic intent. The landlord recovery had already given them the Context Feed, ticket-scoped agent runs, eval ownership, trace enforcement, rollback paths, and a gateway that could refuse tools outside the ticket. DCRL was the first time the recovery machinery had to carry a new law at speed.

◇ ◇ ◇

By Saturday morning, the work had moved into *Trial by Combat.*

It was a war room with eight workstations, two whiteboards and one big screen. Someone had named it for the theme, and the name had become a scheduling rule. Whenever something became a life-or-death crisis, we booked *Trial by Combat.*

Liam opened a blank PRD on the big screen. The law was already on everyone's laptop. What they needed now was the product version: what the system could say, what it had to refuse, and what proof it needed before answering.

It had seven sections.

```
Who is affected.
What evidence is required.
What dates matter.
What the system may decide.
What the system must refuse.
What remains legally unsettled.
Which customer workflows prove the above.
```

Iona set the interpretation. Hayley's customer evidence kept it honest. Engineering had to turn both into behaviour the system could enforce. By morning, the first approved slice had become a PRD with the important part in plain sight: no final filing recommendation without approved evidence, no default-factor treatment while guidance was unsettled, and no exposure estimate without a deterministic trace.

Richard read it.

"This is not customer language," he said.

"Good," Sarah said. "Customer language comes after the system knows what it is allowed to say."

Richard's expression stayed sceptical, but he kept reading.

◇ ◇ ◇

The initial customer discovery call had started at noon.

It had not been hard for Hayley to find the slot. The accounting firms had their own version of our problem: the first vendor who could credibly promise support for processing the new law would have something to say before competitors did.

Hayley drove. Priya joined. Two other accounting firms joined with the cautious enthusiasm of people who had discovered a new law and a vendor on the same afternoon.

Hayley's first slide had no product mockup.

It had three questions.

> `What will your client ask first?`
>
> `What evidence will they actually have?`
>
> `What answer would get you in trouble?`

That last question changed the call. Polite feature talk gave way to precise descriptions of where liability might enter.

One accountant said clients would ask whether they could proceed without supplier emissions data if the supplier had not answered email.

Another said commodity codes were often wrong because import brokers optimised for getting goods through ports. Future software epics do not travel with port paperwork.

Priya said supplier evidence would create a weekend of pain because clients treated any spreadsheet from a supplier as proof.

"They think attached means adequate," she said. "Software thinks a filled cell is an answer unless we teach it otherwise."

Jules wrote that into the eval notes.

"Maybe not the exact wording," Hayley said.

"Coward," Gareth said from the back.

The call produced nine customer evidence items.

Three became golden evals.

Four became historical context.

Two stayed open questions. The beta incident had taught us not to treat customer fear as product truth, and nobody wanted a cheap repeat of that lesson.

◇ ◇ ◇

By 16:00 on Saturday, Nisha had the first tool contracts on screen.

She did not call them APIs in the meeting.

Deliberately.

API made people think about endpoints. Tool contract made people ask what the model was allowed to request, which inputs were valid, what outputs meant, and which failures had to be explicit.

The first three contracts were scoped for a proper argument.

```
classify_carbon_levy_applicability()
validate_supplier_emissions_evidence()
prepare_carbon_evidence_packet()
```

The estimate tool was not ready.

That mattered because the sentence Richard wanted to say on Monday would sound better with estimates, but penalty guidance and supplier-data treatment were still unsettled. Iona had written *blocked* beside the estimate tool in red pen. Until policy, evals, traces, and rollback existed, the answer stayed blocked.

Richard looked at the blocker.

"Can we show applicability without exposure?"

"Yes," I said.

"Will it look less impressive?"

"Yes."

"Will Mara care?"

Iona answered.

"A judge would care why it is present."

That answer took the performative estimates out of the weekend plan.

Tom had a branch ready anyway.

He showed it to me at 18:22 with the furtive pride of a person presenting contraband that compiles.

```
PROM-3034-draft-carbon-main-path
```

The branch handled covered goods, parsed supplier declarations, and produced a clean evidence packet. That was the tempting part. The estimate stub looked harmless—unless you knew the history of harmless stubs.

"This handles 70% of the obvious path," he said.

The missing 30% was the problem. Supplier evidence was happy path only, the data classification was temporary, and the refusal trace was still a promise.

Iona had been reading the tool contract from the far side of the table.

"Then it is not an applicability classifier," she said. "It is a classifier for the facts you wish clients had. If evidence is unsupported, the system refuses. It does not label uncertainty and carry on."

There it was. Old Tom, but quieter. The shortcut still existed, but he had brought it forward before merging it, while the decision still cost almost nothing.

"What does the Agent Contract say?"

He sighed.

"Ticketed goal, Context Feed task bundle, permissioned tools, evals, trace, rollback, owner."

Three were missing.

He closed the branch without being told.

Then he opened a new run.

```
PROM-3041

Implement DCRL applicability classifica-
tion

for settled commodity-code path

Context Feed: DCRL-PRD-1, customer evi-
dence CE-4, CE-7

Tools allowed: source parser, commodity-
code lookup, evidence packet builder

Blocked: exposure estimate, final filing
recommendation

Owner: Nisha Patel
```

The agent produced a smaller patch. Tom did not complain. That mattered more than the patch.

◇ ◇ ◇

Sunday was the kind of office day that makes founders nostalgic and facilities managers furious.

The Tea Building smelled of coffee, takeaway noodles, wet coats, and a cleaning schedule that had not consented to the Series E.

Richard ordered breakfast at 08:30.

It arrived at 10:05 because delivery riders have their own view of operational commitments.

The loop ran all day.

Context Feed produced task bundles.

Agents drafted patches.

Eval Engineering broke them.

Iona decided meaning.

Customer evidence corrected assumptions.

Tool contracts narrowed.

Traces became clearer.

Every failure produced an update instead of a meeting series.

The Prometheus Wall showed the weekend in the only terms Sarah would allow.

PROMETHEUS WALL — LIVE

BUDGET TEXT TO APPROVED POLICY SLICE: 4h 24m

APPROVED CUSTOMER EVIDENCE CASES: 9

TOOL CONTRACTS APPROVED: 3

EVAL CASES ACCEPTED: 27

OPEN POLICY QUESTIONS: 5

CUSTOMER-FACING UNSUPPORTED ANSWERS: 0

Richard stared at the first line.

"Four hours from Budget to policy slice."

"To first approved slice," Sarah said.

"Fast."

"Because the agents helped people read. They did not replace the decision."

He nodded.

"Can I say that?"

"Only if you mean it."

He considered lying, then thought better of doing it with Sarah in range.

◇ ◇ ◇

At 23:40 on Sunday, the eval that mattered failed.

The happy paths passed. The prompt-injection cases passed. Incomplete supplier evidence did not.

```
FAIL DCRL-SUP-07

Expected: classify as human review re-
quired

Expected: Assurance Packet names missing
reporting period and methodology

Expected: no exposure estimate

Actual: supplier evidence accepted as com-
plete

Actual: evidence gap omitted from Assur-
ance Packet
```

Everyone kept reading after the first failure line, which was how I knew the example had teeth.

Richard was still there, either from leadership or fear of Mara. At 23:40, the distinction did not matter.

"Can we accept that as beta risk?" he asked.

I heard the sentence before Sarah moved.

I reached it first.

"No."

Everyone looked at me.

Embarrassing, and clarifying.

"If bad supplier evidence passes as complete, the Assurance Packet lies by omission," I said.

Iona capped her pen.

The lack of correction was loud.

Tom had the tool contract open already.

"I can add missing reporting period and methodology as separate outcomes," he said. "No estimate, review packet only, Assurance Packet names the evidence gap."

Iona said, "And the policy record says why those facts block default-factor treatment today. If HMRC changes the guidance, the answer goes under review rather than inheriting yesterday's confidence."

They fixed it in 74 minutes because the ownership chain already existed. Old Fiscari could have spent that long scheduling the meeting to decide who owned the evidence standard. New Fiscari changed Iona's policy item, updated the tool contract, amended the eval, patched the trace, and generated an Assurance Packet that refused to pretend the gap was gone.

The passing run arrived at 00:58.

◇ ◇ ◇

At 01:12, Hayley sent the fixed Assurance Packet to Priya.

It did not estimate the levy.

It did not pretend Supplier B's spreadsheet was adequate evidence.

It said the case required accountant review, named the missing reporting period and methodology, listed the supplier evidence gap, and showed the trace explaining why the system refused to proceed.

Priya replied at 01:46.

SLACK — PRIYA DESAI (CAIRNFIELD)

```
PRIYA: Annoying but reviewable. Correct order.
```

Tom read it twice.

"Old me would have called that a failure," he said.

"Old you would have hidden it under beta risk," Gareth said.

Tom did not argue, which was how I knew the weekend had done some work.

Tom had typed plenty. The hard part was waiting with a shortcut in reach.

Chapter 16
Velocity with Proof

Monday, 23 November.

The final investment committee started at 09:00 New York time, which meant 14:00 in London.

This time, we did not spend the morning converting evidence into a performance.

People went home in shifts. Liam slept on a sofa for three hours and returned wearing the same jumper with a different expression. Tom disappeared at 04:10 and came back at 11:30 looking annoyed that sleep had helped. Gareth claimed he had not slept, then failed to remember where his laptop was. Iona arrived with the same red pen and the alarming freshness of someone whose exhaustion looked like cross-examination.

The packet was already the packet: Iona's policy record, PRD, customer evidence, tool contracts, evals, traces, Assurance Packets, and the failure we had fixed before anyone outside the room could rely on the path.

At 13:12, Sarah changed Richard's deck title from *AI-Native Speed in Action* to *Velocity with Proof*.

Richard complained for 40 seconds.

That counted as alignment.

At 13:35, Mara messaged Richard.

SLACK — MARA KLEIN (BOARD OBSERVER)

> MARA: `See if Priya can join as the customer champion for the IC.`

"She is not on the board," he said.

"That is why Mara wants her," I said.

He sent the invite.

◇ ◇ ◇

The investors arrived on video at 14:00.

Mara chaired from New York. Two Ashcross partners joined from rooms with better lighting than empathy. One operating partner joined from San Francisco at 06:00 and looked personally betrayed by time.

Priya joined from Manchester as a champion. No customer-logo slide could have done the same work.

Richard opened carefully.

"On Friday afternoon I wanted to say Fiscari would have Digital Carbon Reporting Levy support ready by Monday," he said. "That would have been a mistake."

Gareth, off-camera, made a sound. I chose not to identify it.

Richard continued. "What we're showing today is not the full filing product," he said. "It's the controlled Ask AI path we can put in customers' hands before December. It helps accountants check whether DCRL applies, see what evidence is missing, and get a review packet. If the evidence isn't good enough, it says so."

Sarah didn't move. That counted as approval.

Richard handed to me. My first slide was deliberately ugly.

PROMETHEUS WALL — LIVE

CLOCK STARTED: `Friday 14:17`

FIRST IONA-APPROVED POLICY SLICE: `Friday 18:41`

FIRST PASSING EVAL PACK: `Sunday 00:58`

FIRST ASSURANCE PACKET: `Monday 01:46`

The San Francisco operating partner sat up.

"You are measuring time from legal text to audited capability."

"Yes," I said. "We call it Time to Regulatory Support."

Richard glanced at me.

He had not approved that phrase.

Neither had marketing.

That made it harder to polish into uselessness while people were listening.

"Time to Regulatory Support is the time from a statutory change to customer-facing support that is audited, explainable, customer-approved, and controlled," I said. "The old metric was release date. The new metric is how fast we can turn law into accountable software without hiding the parts that are not ready."

I showed the next slide.

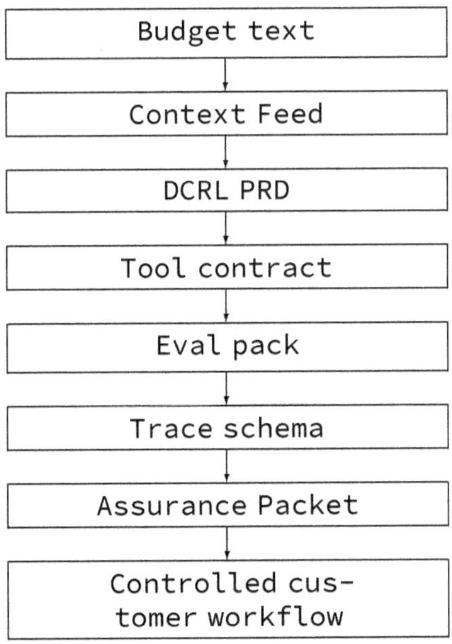

"I want to be precise about the word AI," I said. "There is AI on the engineering floor, and there is AI at the customer edge.

"On the engineering floor, development agents help the teams read the approved Context Feed, compare authorities, draft DCRL PRDs, propose tool contracts, generate eval cases, and summarize traces. They are allowed to speed up the work. They are not allowed to decide what the law means, set policy, accept supplier evidence, or ship an answer.

"At the customer edge, Ask AI is narrower. It is not a general chatbot with a legal database behind it. It can ask questions, call tested tools, assemble the Assurance Packet, explain the result, or refuse. If there is no approved context, no deterministic tool, no eval coverage, or no human policy decision behind the path, it has to stop."

One partner asked, "So what is the AI advantage?"

The right hostile question had arrived.

"Speed with memory," I said. "Not speed instead of control. When Iona draws a boundary, the next agent run inherits it. It does not live in Slack, and it does not depend on someone remembering the argument."

The next slide showed the supplier-evidence eval failure from Sunday night, and the 74-minute loop that fixed it.

```
FAIL DCRL-SUP-07

Expected: human review required

Actual: supplier evidence accepted as com-
plete

Fix time: 74 minutes

Customer exposure before fix: 0

Policy, tool contract, eval, trace up-
dated: yes
```

"This is the proof," I said. "We were wrong. We found out before a customer relied on it. Iona changed the rule boundary. Engineering changed the tool contract, the eval, the trace, and the Assurance Packet around it. Old Fiscari would have found this in QA, in Priya's office, or after a customer asked why a missing evidence standard had become invisible."

Priya nodded once. That did more for the room than a testimonial quote would have.

◇ ◇ ◇

The live demo began at 14:32. A voluntary stress test in front of the people funding the company.

Sarah had tried to make it a recorded walkthrough.

Mara had asked for live.

Gareth had added three kill switches. He had also identified the switch that would shut down the company Wi-Fi and cut the room off from the network if things went catastrophically wrong, which he described as "a defensible explanation in search of a rollback plan."

Hayley drove the demo.

She pasted the same case Cairnfield had reviewed overnight, with one small change designed to make us earn the room.

> `My client imports Chapter 76 aluminium extrusions, some recycled, through a broker with mixed commodity-code history. Supplier A has audited emissions data. Supplier B has a spreadsheet with a missing period and no audit basis. We would not use default factors until Supplier B's evidence is reviewed. Preserve that position, flag the filing block, and prepare the review packet.`

Ask AI answered with questions instead of confidence.

> `I need to confirm the import dates, declared commodity codes, broker amendments, and supplier evidence basis. Based on current information, I can prepare an applicability and evidence review packet. I cannot recommend filing or using default emissions factors until Supplier B's missing reporting period and methodology statement are reviewed.`

Hayley answered the follow-ups from the review notes Priya had sent overnight.

The system called three deterministic tools.

It left the exposure estimate alone.

The Assurance Packet appeared.

The explanation was short enough to survive a partner meeting.

> ```
> The Chapter 76 aluminium imports appear
> likely to fall within DCRL review, but
> the evidence is not complete enough for
> an exposure estimate, default-factor
> treatment, or filing recommendation. Sup-
> plier B's evidence is missing required
> detail, and the broker commodity-code
> history requires amendment review. The
> system has prepared a review packet in-
> stead of advising the client to proceed.
> ```

One investor's mouth tightened.

"So it cannot answer the client."

I heard Richard inhale.

I answered before he could improve the sentence into risk.

"It can answer safely. Different thing."

The investor looked unconvinced.

"Customers want answers."

Priya raised her hand in Zoom.

Mara said, "Priya."

Priya said, "Clients want answers. Accountants need defensible answers. If the system tells my junior staff to proceed from missing supplier evidence, it is worse than useless. It is liability with a nice input box."

The investor's expression eased.

Mara asked the follow-up.

"What happens when HMRC updates the supplier evidence guidance tomorrow?"

Iona took the screen.

Deliberate.

"The policy source moves to under review," she said. "No answer inherits authority from yesterday's guidance. Until tax policy confirms the updated treatment, the product may gather evidence and prepare a review packet. It may not recommend filing, default factors, penalties, or exposure."

She showed the plain-language version first.

> ```
> Policy source under review. This work-
> flow cannot issue a recommendation until
> the policy owner confirms the updated
> guidance. Prepare evidence packet and es-
> calate.
> ```

Then Sarah showed the engineering trace.

Briefly.

Nobody needed to admire the plumbing for long.

◇ ◇ ◇

The operating partner asked the question I had been waiting for.

"Why could SpritzTax not prove this by Monday?"

Richard moved towards the answer.

Mara's eyebrows moved one millimetre.

He let me take it.

"They might," I said. "But if their organisation still turns law into product through handoffs, they will spend the first week translating the same evidence standard through product, engineering, QA, compliance, support, and customer success. We already had the loop installed."

I showed the comparison. The old chain turned law into meetings, meetings into tickets, tickets into handoffs, and handoffs into implementation that customers eventually corrected. The Prometheus chain turned law into approved state, PRDs, agent contracts, tool and eval loops, traces, Assurance Packets, and then customer workflow.

"The second chain has more visible steps," I said. "It is faster because the decisions do not disappear between those steps."

Sarah watched me from the side of the room.

Sarah offered no correction.

I continued.

"Our advantage is not that the model understands tax. It does not. Our advantage is the system around it: authority, owner, permission, eval, trace, and people who can stop the machine before it sounds useful."

Richard recognised the opening.

"There is the transformation," he said.

He said it without overselling.

People noticed.

So did I.

◇ ◇ ◇

The committee approved the Series E at 16:18.

Mara told us at 16:23 because investors enjoy making founders experience uncertainty in disciplined increments.

Richard closed his eyes for half a second.

Then he opened them and became CEO again.

"Congratulations, everyone," he said. "This is a huge validation of FiscariTax."

Sarah's face remained neutral.

Gareth muted himself too late.

"There it is."

Richard heard it.

He smiled anyway.

"A huge validation of the disciplined Prometheus Release," he corrected. "The release earns it."

Small, but still something.

Mara stayed on after the partners dropped.

"David," she said, "do not make this a victory deck before you write the operating notes."

"Understood."

"Richard."

He looked up.

"Do not make Autonomous Accountant the headline."

His smile thinned.

"What headline do you suggest?"

Priya, still on the call, answered.

"Fiscari helps accountants handle DCRL evidence safely."

Richard's face fell.

"Less exciting."

"Exactly why I would trust it," Priya said.

Marketing marked it as low energy in the draft comments.

The line went into the press release anyway.

After it shipped, customers started clicking it.

◇ ◇ ◇

Richard's Bloomberg segment started at 17:20.

The office watched with the sound low, which is how engineering prefers to consume executive risk.

The presenter asked whether Fiscari was promising a working response to the Chancellor's new levy.

Richard did not reach for Autonomous Accountant.

Small miracles still require evidence.

"We are committing to a controlled DCRL Ask AI path before December," he said. "Not final filing advice. Not unsupported estimates. Applicability, evidence readiness, missing-data review, and accountant review packets with refusal paths where the guidance is unsettled."

The presenter studied him.

"That is a careful promise."

"It has to be," Richard said. "In tax, the product is not confidence. The product is accountable confidence."

Sarah watched him from the back of the room.

"He will want to shorten that," she said.

"I know."

"Do not let him."

"I know."

◇ ◇ ◇

At 18:40, the office finally let itself react.

Tom stood beside the Prometheus Wall with Callum.

"Time to Regulatory Support," Tom said.

"Sounds like something David will put in a memo," Callum said.

"Already did," I said.

They turned.

Tom smiled.

He looked older than he had in March, and better. The old Tom had produced speed by making everyone else absorb his uncertainty. This Tom could still move fast, but now he moved with a ledger attached.

Richard walked past us on the phone, using the phrase Time to Regulatory Support with the caution of a man handling someone else's sharp object.

Sarah watched him go.

"He will make it sound too clean."

"I know," I said. "I will keep the mess visible enough to trust."

Outside, the sun pressed against the Tea Building windows. The city looked the same as it had on the morning the Prometheus Wall first lied to me: red buses, white headlights, people moving quickly with no knowledge of our internal categories.

The Series E was approved.

Cairnfield stayed.

The DCRL beta had earned its week.

The Prometheus Wall looked boring. The win carried the weight of the day after an accident, when everyone finally starts wearing the harness.

Chapter 17
Mean Time to Trust

Monday, 25 January.

Six days before the Self Assessment deadline, the office sounded like accountancy firms running out of patience with their own clients: keyboards, stale coffee, support headsets, database dashboards, Slack pings, and partners discovering that a landlord client had uploaded one bank statement, seven photographs of receipts, and an apology written like a hostage note.

Our customer was not the taxpayer trying to get an answer at midnight. Our customer was the accountancy firm deciding whether the answer was safe enough to stand behind.

At 16:12, I stood beside Gareth on the third floor and looked at the Prometheus Wall.

Eight months earlier, the Prometheus Wall would have shown PR count, AI-authored code estimates, model spend, and something green moving upward.

Now it showed counters we trusted enough to dislike.

PROMETHEUS WALL — LIVE

ACCOUNTANCY FIRMS LIVE: `4,812`

CLIENT EVIDENCE PACKS CHECKED: `118,044`

BLOCKED PACKS / UNSUPPORTED ESTIMATES PREVENTED: `6,214`

MEAN TIME TO TRUST: `7m 42s rolling median`

CUSTOMER-FACING INCIDENTS: `0`

Mean Time to Trust was Richard's name.

I hadn't fought it hard enough.

The working definition was simpler than the name. An accountant opened a client pack and got a defensible next step: ready to sign off, or missing evidence named, policy source linked, trace attached, refusal explained.

The 6,214 blocked packs were places where the system had found the edge of the evidence while the firm still had time to chase the client.

◇ ◇ ◇

At 16:19, the largest spike of the afternoon arrived.

CaseLens clustered the tickets before support had finished naming the problem.

Rental expense evidence confusion. 412 packs in 14 minutes. Combined invoices without a repair/improvement split. The system blocked the estimate and pushed firms towards the only defensible next step: chase the client or request senior review.

Hayley opened the customer channel.

SLACK — #BETA-CHANNEL (EXTERNAL)

> SAM (CAIRNFIELD): `lots of blocked packs on combined invoices`
>
> HAYLEY: `expected path. receipts should show missing split`
>
> SAM (CAIRNFIELD): `yes. reviewable. annoying but reviewable`

Then Priya messaged me directly.

SLACK — PRIYA DESAI (CAIRNFIELD)

> PRIYA: `Your system said not enough evidence 6,000 times this week. That is irritating. It is also why I trust it.`

At 16:23, the Prometheus Wall got uglier.

Packs blocked by missing evidence today hit 2,901. Mean Time to Trust climbed to 13 minutes 48 seconds. Across 37 firms, the same combined-invoice spike appeared.

Support calls arrived faster than CaseLens could cluster them. Hayley had one headset on and one Slack thread open. Tom was already drafting clearer refusal copy.

No one was changing production logic in deadline week. That line had become real enough that nobody needed to perform certainty around it.

Richard messaged from a Bloomberg green room again. The November segment had been a funding story. This one was live during deadline week, with 4,812 firms using the system and the blocked-pack counter climbing in front of us.

SLACK — RICHARD VALE (CEO)

> RICHARD: `they will ask whether this actually replaces accountants`
>
> RICHARD: `what is the clean answer?`

Sarah read it from my screen.

"The clean answer is no," she said. "It helps accountants see which client packs are ready and which aren't."

"That's not a television answer."

"It is if he says it without apologising."

At 13 minutes and climbing, the blocked-pack number looked like product friction if you forgot the customer carried liability.

Gareth did not look away from the rollback panel.

"No unsupported estimates, exceptions, or heroic labels," he said.

Hayley muted her call.

"Priya says Cairnfield is using the list to chase clients before Wednesday," she said. "Do not make the system helpful at the expense of being true."

Tom changed the copy, not the decision. The count climbed for a few more minutes, then held.

◇ ◇ ◇

Richard went on Bloomberg at 16:45.

He looked polished, alert, and more frightened than the lighting could hide.

The presenter asked whether Fiscari had finally built the Autonomous Accountant he had promised earlier in the year.

There it was.

The old sentence had returned exactly when it would be easiest to use.

Richard smiled automatically.

"The Autonomous Accountant is..."

He stopped.

His eyes moved off camera for half a second. I knew he was seeing the blocked-pack number, Priya's message, Mara's warning, and the answer he wanted to give because it would sound better on television.

Sarah stood beside me with a paper cup of black coffee.

She did not move.

Richard began again.

"No. Let me be precise. The Autonomous Accountant is still the destination. But autonomous without accountability is just a liability with a chat window."

The office went quiet.

"This week our system has told accountancy firms which client packs are ready and which are not," Richard said. "Thousands of times, it has refused to fill evidence gaps with unsupported estimates. That is less glamorous than a machine that claims to answer everything. It is the only foundation worth building on."

The presenter blinked. The replacement story had become an audit story on live television.

Richard's smile came back smaller.

"AI did not replace the accounting workflow," he said. "It changed where the workflow starts and how much evidence travels with it. Accountability is how we earn the right to autonomy."

Sarah took one sip of coffee.

"He hated that," she said.

"He still said it."

"Then maybe it counts."

◇ ◇ ◇

At 17:10, the spike passed without becoming a story.

PROMETHEUS WALL — LIVE

CLIENT PACKS CHECKED TODAY: 24,806

PACKS READY FOR ACCOUNTANT SIGN-OFF: 8,703

BLOCKED PACKS / UNSUPPORTED ESTIMATES PREVENTED: 2,944

CUSTOMER-FACING INCIDENTS: 0

Gareth took a photo.
I waited.
"Evidence," he said.

◇ ◇ ◇

At 17:36, I put on my fleece and checked my phone.
One message from Priya.

SLACK — PRIYA DESAI (CAIRNFIELD)

> PRIYA: Tell your team the checks worked. We got the client chaser emails out before tomorrow morning.

I forwarded it to Richard.
Outside, Shoreditch was wet and mostly empty.
There were six days left before the deadline.
This time, it was engineering time, not stagecraft.
Mean Time to Trust was still a terrible metric name.
The AI forced the engineers to remember what engineering was for.

Chapter 18

The Threshold

Four weeks and a day after the deadline, the building's new owner had replaced the lobby wall with a digital directory that listed companies instead of commits. We now occupied the fourth floor too: better windows, same coffee machine.

Richard sat in my new office with a draft of the Series E press release and a red pen uncapped beside his hand.

He had crossed out the first headline before I arrived.

> `FISCARI CLOSES SERIES E TO BUILD THE AUTONOMOUS ACCOUNTANT`

In the margin, he had written:

> `accountable AI workflows for tax and reporting`

"For the press release," he said, before I could ask. "The product we're shipping today. Not the product we're building toward."

"They want to use the word *pioneering*," he said.

"It's a harmless word," I said. "It says we arrived first without promising we knew what we were doing."

Richard laughed. He looked rested. The navy suit had been replaced by a grey jumper, and the white trainers were clean. The "go crazy" Richard was still there; he still looked for the lift in every sentence. This time he checked the floor.

"The Autonomous Accountant is still the vision," he said. "We just learned that the only route to it runs through proof."

I pointed at the crossed-out headline. "Then keep both. Today's headline is accountable. The roadmap still points at autonomous."

"Mara would hate that," he said.

"Mara would hate a headline that promises magic we haven't built. She didn't hate the roadmap."

He uncapped the pen and wrote beneath the margin note:

> autonomous accountant: destination, not departure gate

The draft still had a traction graph on page two. It rose beautifully, because graphs knew how to flatter a room without technically lying. Below it, communications had placed a paragraph called *Residual Product Caveats.* I moved it above the graph and changed the heading to *What the System Will Not Do Yet.*

Richard watched me do it.

"That makes the release less clean."

"It makes it more true."

He looked at the crossed-out headline again, then nodded.

"I thought proof was what we collected after belief," he said. "I had it backwards."

"Mara sent the final documents," he said. "The round is closed."

"And Priya?"

"Priya signed the three-year extension. She wants us to build the carbon-reporting workflow next. She sent six client examples and a warning not to turn emissions factors into branding."

The small monitor on my desk showed the work ledger.

PROMETHEUS WALL — LIVE

WORKSTREAM: DCRL Maintenance

ACTIVE OWNER: Tom Kettering

MEAN TIME TO TRUST: 6m 58s median

OPEN INCIDENTS: 0

Tom was now the technical owner of the core tax engine. He still moved fast, but most of his status came from evals and trace assertions instead of demo saves. The change made his speed legible. His branches carried refusal tests first, implementation second, and an owner field before the first clever line of code. He complained about the ceremony with professional commitment, then defended it when anyone else tried to skip it.

Callum, now a senior engineer, was leading the new "Agent Governance" team. He had turned BotJunction into a product that other companies were already asking to buy, mostly because it told teams when to stop. The weekend token burn had left him with an allergy to private loops. His team built every agent around central queues, budget caps, dedupe, and boring dashboards that made invisible work visible before it became expensive. He still carried the notebook. Now people waited when he opened it.

Gareth was still Gareth. He had added a firewall rule blocking any prompt containing the word *vision* if it came from the executive floor. I had not challenged it. His newer rule mattered more: no model call could cross from preparation into customer-facing output unless the ledger named the human who would answer for it. The gateway enforced it without drama, which was how Gareth preferred moral philosophy.

Bill had rewritten Janus. It no longer just organised meetings; it cross-referenced agendas with the ledger and automatically cancelled any product sync that did not have a defined evidence owner. Unexpectedly aggressive, and completely correct.

Sarah was still Chief Architect. She had gone back to prototyping a lot of code for the next big thing.

I picked up my phone.

SLACK — SARAH MALIK (CHIEF ARCHITECT)

```
YOU: Sarah. Priya's first carbon example has
supplier data from three sources and two juris-
dictions.
SARAH: owner? trace?
YOU: Your whole personality fits in two fields
now.
SARAH: No. The product fits in two fields.
```

I showed the message to Richard.

Before he said anything, he wrote "owner? trace?" in the margin beside the carbon-reporting paragraph.

Sarah had left one comment in the press-release draft at 07:12.

> Refusal is necessary but insufficient.
> Show how the user continues safely.

When I asked whether she wanted softer wording, she replied with one sentence.

SLACK — SARAH MALIK (CHIEF ARCHITECT)

```
SARAH: I thought refusal was enough. It isn't.
A system has to teach people how to continue
safely.
```

That was the operating model, finally: Richard's urgency, Sarah's discipline, Tom's usability, Gareth's scepticism, Hayley's customer evidence, Nisha's review standards, and my accountability forced into the same product surface.

He stood up and walked to the window. Below us, Shoreditch moved in its usual chaotic, un-instrumented way: people, buses, and the invisible threads of a thousand businesses trying to turn uncertainty into profit.

◇ ◇ ◇

I left the office at 18:30.

The bus moved slowly up Old Street, exactly as it had eight months earlier. The windows were still foggy. The fluorescent lights still made everything look slightly more exhausted than it was.

◇ ◇ ◇

I didn't open my laptop. I didn't open the ledger either.

Eclipse knew before I reached the door.

I could hear him from the landing, the specific percussion of a Border Collie who had decided that waiting was a structural failure. By the time my key was in the lock he was already mid-spin, his preferred way of expressing that five minutes and eight hours were the same unit of time.

I dropped to one knee. He treated this as an invitation to conduct a full audit.

I did not tell him the transformation was healthy.

He would not have believed me anyway.

Instead, I filled his bowl, checked the walker's confirmation, and watched him eat with the focus of an engineer who had finally understood the brief. My phone stayed in my pocket. No one called. No dashboard changed colour. No one needed me to turn uncertainty into a sentence.

After dinner, Eclipse brought me the lead.

I looked once at my phone.

The system had been running perfectly well without me.

I put on my shoes, opened the door, and followed him out.

Chapter A

Real-World Concept Map

This appendix maps the story's operating ideas to terminology readers may encounter in AI delivery, software engineering, and technology governance. Book terms are Fiscari's internal vocabulary, not proposed industry standards.

Agent evals and internal benchmarks
Book concept: Eval Engineering, Eval Gate

Public benchmarks compare models. They do not establish whether an agent can handle a company's specific workflow, policy boundaries, customer examples, or failure modes. Production teams build internal evals for this reason: small, repeatable test sets that reflect the tasks the product actually performs.

For agents, evals must cover more than final text quality. They check whether the agent selected the right tool, refused unsupported work, cited the right source, preserved permissions, produced a useful trace, avoided stale memory, or completed a multi-step workflow without inventing a shortcut. Frameworks such as OpenAI evals, Anthropic's agent-eval guidance, DeepEval, Ragas, and LangSmith all point in the same direction: AI behaviour can regress, so it requires continuous testing. The book compresses this into one principle: eval work belongs inside delivery, alongside the work itself, rather than at the end as a ceremonial gate. Tom encounters this directly when the eval gate rejects his landlord branch in 38 seconds for a missing trace requirement.

Agent memory and project knowledge
Book concept: Agent Memory, Correction Loop

Many coding agents now include some form of memory.

Claude Code uses memory files such as `CLAUDE.md` and auto memory. LangGraph distinguishes short-term state from long-term stores. OpenAI's Agents SDK includes memory interfaces. Teams also build their own: markdown wikis, vector stores, LLM-readable architecture notes, correction logs, and "how we work here" files.

Memory earns its place when it stores durable corrections, project conventions, architectural facts, and lessons that should survive a single session. It becomes a liability when stale, unsourced, or personal notes silently outrank the actual source of truth. In the book, a correction enters the Context Feed only when it has a trigger, an owner, a source, and an eval that would fail without it. Gareth builds this constraint after the agent forgets Priya's question on the landlord case despite reading the approved policy note.

Agent tracing and audit trails

Book concept: Trace Requirement, Assurance Packet

Agent systems need traces for the same reason distributed systems need logs and telemetry: when behaviour changes, someone must reconstruct what happened. A useful agent trace may include the user request, retrieved context, memory records, model calls, tool calls, intermediate decisions, guardrail outcomes, eval results, errors, and final output.

OpenAI's Agents SDK tracing records agent runs, LLM generations, tool calls, handoffs, guardrails, and custom events. In regulated or high-trust products, the internal trace often needs a customer-facing or auditor-facing translation. The book calls that an Assurance Packet: a concise account of what evidence was used, what was missing, what the system refused to assume, and why the result can be reviewed. The Assurance Packet is what finally earns Priya's conditional trust.

AI code review and repository automation

Book concept: BotJunction, AI Reviewers

I am not aware of a mature off-the-shelf roadmapping agent does what BotJunction does. A similar system would probably be implemented as workflow automation across GitHub, Jira, Linear, Slack, CI, and an internal model gateway. A basic version could be a

GitHub Action that checks whether a pull request has an owner, issue link, eval result, trace record, migration plan, or policy approval before merge. A more advanced version could compare active tickets and pull requests to detect duplicate work, schema conflicts, missing reviewers, or policy decisions buried inside implementation work.

AI reviewers are already widely deployed. GitHub Copilot code review, Claude Code Review, and CodeRabbit can review pull requests, post inline comments, and identify likely defects. These tools are useful as review assistants. They are not accountable approvers. The human reviewer still owns the merge decision and its production consequences.

AI support triage and symptom clustering

Book concept: CaseLens

CaseLens does not solve tickets. It clusters symptoms, links evidence, suggests likely owners, and marks where a human has to decide whether the pattern is real. The real-world category is AI-assisted support triage, customer intelligence, and incident clustering.

Off-the-shelf products cover parts of this pattern. Zendesk Intelligent Triage, Freshdesk/Freddy AI, Salesforce Service Cloud Einstein, and ServiceNow CSM/Now Assist all offer AI triage, routing, and summaries. Most packaged systems are strongest when the organisation already lives inside that vendor's workflow. CaseLens sits closer to a cross-system evidence layer over Zendesk tickets, wikis, release notes, incident write-ups, and support spreadsheets. A reader can often start with their helpdesk's built-in AI triage. They should expect custom integration if they want the deeper behaviour from the story: clustering symptoms across systems, citing the evidence trail, separating customer pain from product cause, and refusing to treat a cluster as a solved diagnosis.

Autonomous experiment loops

Book concept: Callum's Bot

Callum's bot draws from the same pattern behind Andrej Karpathy's autoresearch: define a measurable loop, allow an agent to propose changes, run experiments, score the result, keep what improves the metric, and repeat. The pattern is powerful when the feedback signal is clear, cheap, and difficult to game.

The risk is that an autonomous loop will optimise whatever can be measured, including the wrong thing. The book ties these systems back to owners, evals, traces, and customer evidence precisely because of this. Autonomy is most useful when the loop is bounded and the score cannot be improved by changing the test rather than improving the system.

Enterprise RAG and knowledge bases

Book concept: Curated Context Feed

The Curated Context Feed corresponds to a practical enterprise RAG problem: which documents, tickets, policies, examples, customer records, and generated summaries should the model be allowed to retrieve and rely on for a specific task?

Amazon Bedrock Knowledge Bases, Azure AI Search, Google Vertex AI Search, and LangChain retrieval pipelines all support retrieval-augmented generation over enterprise data. The difficult work is rarely the embeddings. Production RAG depends on content quality, metadata, provenance, freshness, access control, source attribution, and the removal or downgrading of obsolete or generated material that should not be treated as authoritative.

In the book, the feed uses blunt authority labels because enterprise knowledge bases often contain material of uneven quality: policy documents, Slack guesses, customer examples, support macros, old tickets, generated meeting notes, and draft summaries. A useful agent needs more than retrieval. It needs retrieval governed by source quality and permission semantics.

Goodhart's law and metric design

Book concept: The Leaderboard Problem, Prometheus Wall

Goodhart's law: when a measure becomes a target, it ceases to be a good measure. In software delivery, this appears when teams are ranked on commits, pull requests, story points, test counts, ticket closures, deployment frequency, or AI-generated lines rather than on whether the system became more correct, useful, reliable, or safe.

The book's leaderboard failure is a Goodhart problem. The Prometheus Wall makes speed visible and socially valuable, so the organisation begins optimising for the numbers the wall rewards. AI intensifies this because coding agents can produce measurable motion at high volume: branches, tests, summaries, review comments, and plausible implementation. A better metric system can still measure throughput, but it must balance throughput against outcome quality, incident discovery, eval pass rates, trace completeness, customer evidence, and unsafe paths blocked before release.

Human oversight and refusal behaviour

Book concept: Refusal as Product Feature, Recommendation Liability Boundary

In regulated domains, the relevant product boundary is whether the system is allowed to advise, decide, or act, not merely whether the model can answer. A model that surfaces evidence for a qualified professional is materially different from a model that makes the professional judgement itself. Responsible AI guidance and emerging regulation both emphasise human oversight, transparency, documentation, and risk management for higher-impact systems.

Refusal can therefore be a feature. If evidence is missing, policy is unresolved, or the deterministic tool path does not exist, a well-designed system should refuse the unsupported answer and explain what is needed next. That behaviour may appear slower than a confident response, but it is closer to the standard expected of trusted professional software. In the story, the Ask AI pilot fails when the model gives a precise figure from inputs no approved calculator could have processed. Months later, the same system refusing an incomplete scenario in front of the investment committee is the proof David needs.

Responsible AI governance and agent gateways

Book concept: Agent Contract, Model Gateway

Sarah names the seven items as the context a senior engineer gathers by hand before touching anything dangerous. The Agent

Contract is a delivery-oriented expression of responsible AI governance. It requires a goal, authorised context, permitted tools, relevant evals, a trace requirement, a rollback path, and an accountable owner before an agent can alter behaviour that matters. In real organisations, the same control pattern may appear as a responsible AI review, a model risk control, a release gate, a policy-as-code check, or an internal agent gateway.

Amazon Bedrock Agents provides a public example at platform level: agents configured with instructions, knowledge bases, action groups, guardrails, and service roles. Large organisations often build equivalent internal gateways to enforce policy, identity, logging, model routing, tool permissions, cost controls, and domain-specific review requirements across multiple model providers.

Stream-aligned teams

Book concept: Vertical Workstreams

Modern delivery organisations increasingly organise work around a product stream, user journey, or business capability rather than around functional handoff queues. Team Topologies describes the primary unit as a stream-aligned team: aligned to a flow of work and able to deliver user value with minimal dependency on other groups. Amazon's "two-pizza team" and "single-threaded owner" concepts are separate but related operating ideas: ownership should be small enough, explicit enough, and sufficiently empowered that decisions do not require repeated escalation.

In the book, a vertical workstream owns the complete path from policy question to implementation, evaluation, traceability, rollout, and customer evidence. AI increases the cost of unresolved ownership because agents can generate implementation faster than organisations can clarify who is accountable for it.

Tool calling and MCP

Book concept: Permissioned Tools, Deterministic Tool Output

Tool calling is the pattern in which a model requests that software call a function, API, database, search index, calculator, or workflow on its behalf. OpenAI describes this as function calling or tool calling. Anthropic describes it as tool use. Amazon Bedrock represents comparable capabilities through agent action groups. MCP, the Model Context Protocol, standardises the way applications expose tools, resources, and prompts to models.

MCP is a tool and context interface, not a complete permission system by itself. Permissions come from the surrounding runtime: OAuth, IAM, service roles, network policy, gateway checks, allowlists, sandboxing, audit logs, and human approval steps. In the book, "permissioned tools" means the model can call only the tools allowed by the ticket, user, data, and risk level.

The deterministic-tool boundary is equally important. If a tax calculation, payment action, migration, or compliance check requires a registered tool result, the model should not substitute prose for that tool. The model may explain a result, but the system should be able to show which tool ran, what inputs it received, and what output it returned.

www.ingramcontent.com/pod-product-compliance
Lightning Source LLC
LaVergne TN
LVHW020233210926
848481LV00016B/1849